In Plain Air

In Plain Air
Poems 1958-1980

Alan Stephens

And let me in these Shades compose
Something in Verse as true as Prose.

Swallow Press
Ohio University Press
Chicago   Athens, Ohio   London

Acknowledgements: Of the later poems in this collection (those written since *Tree Meditation and Others*) some have appeared in *The Southern Review*, *The Denver Quarterly*, *Spectrum*, and *Ondas*.

Swallow Press Books
are published by
Ohio University Press
Athens, Ohio

Library of Congress Cataloging in Publication Data

Stephens, Alan Archer, 1925-
   In plain air.

   I.   Title.
PS3537.T347I5   1982   811'.54   81-22533
ISBN 0-8040-0379-3   AACR2
ISBN 0-8040-0380-7 (pbk.)

for Fran and Alan and Dan and Tim

Contents

Note

Years pass and there continues in me a preoccupation
with what it is to be in the physical universe, with its
always individual near-at-hand doings and beings,
human and otherwise; the whole show shading off into
immensity and vagueness, and (however splendid or
frightful or dull or, ultimately, unimaginably strange)
with its bare unrelenting factuality hurtling along
impassively as it does, in a kind of final dignity. Some
sense of this preceded by a long time the writing of the
poems, I suppose, and has something to do with their
unreconstructed realism and particularity.

The poems are nonetheless meditations, and, as I said
about some of them in another place, where descriptive
they are descriptive meditations, and not meditative
descriptions.

Something else. Among the new poems are poems I
wouldn't let out by themselves but that—like an
"openwork" line in a stanza—make their contribution to
the ensemble: what counts for me in any collection is less
the individual poem than the individual life, finding its
way somehow, anyhow, directly and otherwise, into the
whole work.

A few of the previously published poems have been
revised—mostly changes of a word or phrase, a few
slightly more extensive, none meant to affect the original
substance of the poem but only to remove or make less
evident some local blemish.

A.S.

Winter Dusks

Autumn: Island
(after Jorge Guillén)

Autumn, an island
with a severe
profile, watches the combers with their crests
that waver, race forward
to their glistening destruction.

A love for line, and
the grapevine is stripped
of its overlapping green

and a small basket
filled with clusters
out of—good luck: sealed in them
a balancing of dreams
about things possible.

From secret high spirits
a clean style; wisdom the more definite
as it becomes the more inconspicuous, a plain
branch above the hurrying colors—

now in this October
and afternoon light
where a bright leaf
of the persimmon has just launched itself
abruptly from a twig end

now in this clear, still air
where the mountain road curves off
up ahead, dropping
and lifting sharply

_____ at Eighty-Six

This last photograph, for the book jacket,
and you the next thing to the corpse

you will be in a month or so,
the abundant white hair stiff and dull,

the shadows black and sharp in a face now
papery skin over bird-bone; here's

a condescending Introduction by a principal
silly ass of the current literary scene.

Never mind, never mind! it chill
and nearly dark now, and you the vesper sparrow

still twittering! no matter that the twittering's weak
and repetitive, in the black locust tree

that holds its thorny old branches, iron hard, above
the frozen ground you criss-crossed when young; winter
    fields,

bare and rolling, run to the dark East, where shines
through trees a long familiar house light;

but here, it's you and the dusk, and a gaunt God
with his speculations, joining you now—the three

of you plenty of company for one another.

The Fall Plowing Back Home: Dozing Off

Young, and I burned the world away,
Ahead of me, anywhere I went,
With my personal blaze.

Now the world is filling back in.
How I like the plain details,
Complete with shadows, in the low sunlight.

When did I empty? —it's as quiet in here
As a cobweb furred with dust.
Let the harness on its peg

Harden, let the green build up
On the battered brass knobs of the hames.
This old manure scent is dry, and very fine.

Long blades of the afternoon
Slope in through the dropsiding,
Slit the dimness. The light wind

Of late afternoon carries clearly
The fly-buzz of a whole fleet
Of tractors, over the flat, brown fields.

The Man of Feeling

Let it go on, he says,
The sweet, steady humming
Of time, and leans again
In the light of the lamp, outside
The gray and dripping day,
Its light entering the window and setting
Its pewter colored shine
On the back of his hand, his books
In reach, the three or four people
He loves best, at their own doings
In the near middle distance
Of his life this wintry day
As he enters his fiftieth year,
Let it go on,
That sweet hum, let there be
No end to it, ever.

*

Curious how ready he is to die
At moments when he looks around
Quite happy with things—driving
Through town this afternoon,
Heading home, looking forward
To dinner and the evening with *her*,
The town so pleasant in the clear, late light
Reflected from the white undersides of clouds
Pushing out over the rooftops
From the mountains, the air
Chill, fresh off the ocean—

At Los Olivos and Alameda Padre Serra

Below St. Mary's retreat
In its greenery, on its hill,
Are some unowned olive trees
Backed by a stone wall
In a crook of the busy street.
You can visit them when you please.

Though trucks gear down and brake,
Growling and hissing, and cars
Whoosh by the place all day,
The light's clear there, the gray
Grove whitens, when it stirs,
As if for its own sake,

The ground is packed and bare
And stained bright purple and black
From the unpicked bitter fruit
That spurt from underfoot.
Walking, I do not lack
For quiet in that air.

                    *

Winter dusk, and I peer
From the stone bridge nearby
Through alder and sycamore
At the stream racing high
And red with mountain mud
And listen till I hear
Under the water-roar
The streambed boulders thud

And see them gone dead white
And silent at this spot,
And the last pool sunk from sight,
And the clear, weightless current
Of the air quivering hot
Over the solid torrent.

                *

A place being manifold
With more than the eye can hold,
Was I once Spanish or Greek
To like these gray trees so—
Or a solitary kid
From the dusty plains,
Much to wonder about
Inside himself and out,
Sent to school in town,
Shown a few things to know,
While, in a country drowse,
All but completely lost—
Who came at last to seek
Clearness in all he did,
And had for all his pains
The thing in itself clear
And the meaning disappear
—A strange curse to bring down
On much that he loved most;
Latterly come to stray
Under these twisted boughs
Of the old wisdom, where
Mixing leaves with air
Off the Sea below
This is what they say—

Σοφία first was skill,
What a craftsman knew,
Physician, sculptor, smith,
And it is so still,
Being just a way
Not a thing to keep
Or a state of mind
That we stiffen with
And go slowly blind—
But an act of mind
In the course of being,
Going with our seeing;
To sit still and know
Is itself to do,
In our moving through
With the rest of things;
Standing here, we go,
Passing we stand still
(So the gray grove sings
Whitening on its hill)
Till at last we see
Or rather, learn to guess
In our doubleness,
That awake we sleep,
Sleeping we're awake,
And all these mixtures mean
That no thing can be
For its own sweet sake;
Clearness has its source
In the Vague and Vast—
Shapeless, these two last,
While clearness's green leaf
Shapely bright and brief

Consummates their powers;
That the seen and unseen
Send into each other
One another's force,
Separated die
Quicker than cut flowers—
As for what you write
(Rustles one old tree)
Why, Athene knows
Every poem goes
No matter at what height
Over rails of prose,
Length on length on length
Shoved by smoky strength
Straight and smooth and bright,
And the ugliness
Where the iron is mined
Of necessity,
Has a dignity
She could not but bless
—If she, brought to birth
By Hephaestus' axe,
Shouting her war cry,
And without a mother,
Were the blessing kind.

*

Such is what I heard
When the branches stirred
In their dialect;
Now I look around
And this bare dry ground
Prompts me to reflect

No man walks beside
Athene the clear-eyed,
She was born complete
Of the bright-lit myth
Where she keeps her distance
From the shadowed earth;
From the twisted trees
Standing here, for instance,
Catching the sea breeze—
Slow to grow and bear,
Whether here or elsewhere
Cultivated stocks
Grafted to the wild
(Mixture in the shoot)
Able to hold out
For the dusty farmer
Through the longest drought,
Grappled in the rocks;
The black, bitter fruit
Yielding a clear oil
That once symboled human
Plenty and good will,
Bitter turning mild
In the hands of skill
For the kind of peace
Households need—all this
Sponsored by a woman
Who was born in armor
And who bore no child.

Mid-October

And such
things as he achieved are
to him now as its ringed
wood to an old tree, firm
and of the essence
and utterly remote
from the present quick
movements of the leaves, whereas
from the most recent
of a varied assortment
of misjudgments in the life
the pain is as keen
as it is familiar, joining
the life's quite particular
griefs that, subsiding of course
in time, run fresh nevertheless
as when, years back,
they arose, while it is now, now
with the first cold wind
of the fall blowing
down the empty road
that he's walking, one more
aging man, lights
from the house windows
piercing now here now there
the wind-roughed trees,
the first leaves
to be torn loose in the season
skidding wildly past him,
he gaining the hilltop,
looking across the canyon

at the mountain, trickling
head-lights along its road,
the trees roaring now and
dark below, their wrenching
tops catching the red
of a last flare of the sunset.
No car passes. Nobody else
out here. The wind hurries
its new, clean, cold volumes of air
through the big vacancy between him
and the mountain: old elation,
come of this icy freshness
in things in their clearness,
shapes—in the sharp air
of this one deepening dusk—black
now and unreturning,
though a man travels
no more than a tree.

Night-Piece

Last night I lay awake
beside my sleeping wife
at four a.m., and listened:
wind sifted through the pine tree
and made a branch tip finger
the roof above our bed
as if reflectively.
Then I went in my mind
the way the wind was taking—
down through the winding canyon,
shouldering past the trees,
and onto Hendry's beach,
across the channel waters,
gaining the channel islands,
and then the open sea
and moving by itself
over the dark swells
and nothing more to seek.

*

My dear slept on beside me
I knew; I had for proof
her light breath on my cheek.
The branch kept fingering
the same place on the roof.

A Light Rain in the Late Evening

A green bush in the shower
That bleared the window pane
Stood shining when it stopped
In its new skin of rain:
While leaves and eaves dripdropped
I stepped out on the scene
To breathe the late cold air,
When the sun broke through again
Forming a leaf of light
On every leaf of green
Making a bush of light
Still green with all its power
In the approach of night
And I could find nowhere
To put the credit for this
And similar unsought pleasures
Various in their measures
In things that barely mattered
That I never thought to keep
And certainly can't miss
When I dissolve in sleep
Leaving them where they're scattered

A Puff of Smoke

A Puff of Smoke

When my old friend writes to me
Of 'the stark fact that the mind
Appears to be infinite
And to have nothing to do
With the scientific "law"
Of dispersion'—I don't know,
I'll have to write in reply,
Maybe it is infinite
As the world of numbers is,
His purlieu. Immortal, though?
Why, it's an activity,

And it stops. Smashing the skull
Ends it—the anesthetist
Interrupts it, telling you
Mildly, 'Let me see how wide
You can open your mouth, now,'
And the next thing is a flood
Of bright gray light, followed not
By immersion in darkness,
But a moment's consciousness
That the light is gone; and then
Not even darkness. Nothing.

What is this nothing? Nothing.
Where is this nothing? . . . Think how
When a reader finishes
His reading, as an event
Of his attention it is
A memory—a different
Event. His book's an object,
Gathers dust among objects

In no terrible darkness
Or emptiness, but only
In things around, continuing.

There are no gaps in the world.
If spirit's intermittent,
A flickerer that at last
Goes out, the body goes on,
Disintegrating only
To other bodies. The fine
Chemicals . . . ! (while the body
And its habitat were what
Spirit had burned for its warmth
And light. In the beginning,
Spontaneous combustion.)

*

—Conscious again; shaking, cold,
Interstellar cold sunk in
To the middle of the bones.
No doubt from the shock. A new
Numbness down there, and fresh pain,
And a meek feebleness, and
Morphine, all teach the spirit
How it sits reliantly,
Precariously, astride
Its old mule, the body, now
Tottering along strange roads.

I am still musing upon
The horrors that shape themselves
In the gray country of drained
Vitality, foul places

And presences that we two
Innocents visited, with
A sighting one night (eyes closed)
Of death's door, going past it
In the hospital basement:
Bare concrete, tall, wide, unmarked,
Set flush in the concrete wall.

     *

The stunned spirit monitors
The shocked and wounded body
And itself; and puzzles how
The mind includes the body
The body includes the mind
Equally.
       —I remember
Using the body the way
One drove a car when a kid:
To see what it could take, from
A curiosity quite
Disinterested, from anger

At a world so impassive
And clearly uninterested
In the spiritual (no
We would not have used that word)
Authority of energies
Our own yet not our own; and
From exuberance . . . . When young
We are I think but distantly
Attached to our bodies, being
Ill-informed still on any
Necessity we live by.

Years pass and we sink into
The body. Now warily there
I find I take a kindly
Interest in the more or less
Faithful old mount (that is
When fairly healthy), wrily
Admiring its survival
Of pain sickness and danger,
With recollections of work,
Food, sleep, love, talk; of places
Where for moments all was well.

And one day we are body,
And nothing more. Though spirit
Is instructed by the body
Not the other way around,
It's in the spirit only
That instruction can take place
—Of what grand elaborate sorts—
While a definition of
The body might be: What knows,
Really knows its lessons, so
Is a fully accredited

Member of the cosmos. While
The spirit, born ignorant
Of its own rules, and the world's,
At the end has, at best, earned
Only a provisional,
Temporary membership,
Still more ignorant than not
(Which must befit it, must be
Of its nature)—and at worst

Will be all but blackballed (yet
Never quite, even at worst?) . . . .

*

Home again! I write my friend,
And at such a time as this—
To be driven home and see
On the way people's fruit trees
Bright with blossoms in back yards;
And on the hills above town
New green from the recent rains
After a dry winter; that
Was a piece of good timing
I tell you; and once at home
Green fresh outside the windows.

*

Still, what the wan spirit knows,
After its late adventures,
Is a world surrounding it
As nicely put together,
And frail, as the seed crown of
A dandelion: and I walk,
Gaining strength, the grassy hills
Through the wild flowers, little
Fire shapes in the green, fading
Here and there with the approach
Of summer, and its routines.

———————

First Deposition

A trout stream in the high Rockies,
my wife's laughter, a little brass whale
from Taiwan, the sight from my study window
of the two blue hills above the trees,
all kinds of cats, the high desert
of northern Nevada, all particulars
concerning the life and writings of Pope,
the time of sundown and just after,
the grammar of any language, a flawless
sea urchin shell found on Hendry's beach
and kept around and looked at
almost daily for ten years now,
all the birds, the look of Greek on the page,
cottonwood trees in summer, glistening
above the ditches in the dry country
of the west, the words of English songs
of the period 1580 to 1620,
the smell of lumber, of the iron
in a hoe as you file it, of a horse;
bolts of fine woolen goods;
the Indian head nickel; rain,
snow, sunshine, wind, darkness,
the game of poker, discovering used bookstores
in large cities, the clear recollection
of the house and farmyard of early childhood,
driving through streets to meet someone
at the airport, at an hour, late or early,
when you are not usually out; bare trees,
the rhythms of iambic trimeter;
granite boulders; coffee; the coming
of the early darkness of December.

Work

Pure Perception

And I woke up this morning
    To nothing on my mind.
Friends, it was putting to your ear a watch
    You had forgot to wind.

It was walking through the half dark
    Of a sales barn after the sale;
Litter and echo; light from a far door
    Falling still and pale—

Was the barren clarity
    Of a February sun
And you look up at a stony peak and see
    That the stone is stone.

O all day long the air
    Will move clear, cold, and thin
Over things that have come up too near to me—
    It will razor off my skin,
    And no event within.

The Weather Man

Cold and from the wrong direction
a cutting wind out of a raw
blue sky, the feelings have shrunk back
and frozen, a swamp iron-hard in the cold,
all the lively emotions of yesterday
not even a memory, but like hearsay.
My brain's been taken out. All day
I go about my duties as usual
with a headful of icy air.

The Gnomes

Months pass and still
they come squeezing out—
little deformed pre-poems
between crammed duties
and whatnot, the attention
wrenched this way and that.

Keeping their distance
they look at me
with their lopsided faces, one eye
higher than the other,
in those eyes the light,
a pale, clear green,
of an unworldly
wisdom; they stand there quietly
for as long as I look at them.

Work

And I wake up,
yeh, it is dawn,
the young helper, waiting
pale and serious
outside the window.

Inside Inside

The Japanese farmer
in Rexroth's translation
hoes weeds all day
and then hoes them again
all night in his dreams

joining a memory of hoeing all day
forty years back, and all night
dreaming of hoeing
till I was so tired in my dream
I found a pile of gunny sacks
in the noon shade of the tree
between the well pump and the garage
and sank down on them and slept,
a dreamless sleeper in a dreaming sleeper.

Late Song: Ambush

I see my bones lie white
And shining in the Light,
I need the darkness here
Inside me to repair
Old purposes much frayed,
Or shelved, being so ill-made,
Parts of my life now broken
For clear thoughts left unspoken,
Things I uttered, too,
Made some of it run untrue,
Of all that's mine alone
Little fit to be shown—
With more work crowding in,
A fresh page to begin,
And a recent bad mistake
To fix, lest the Light break
And my case still not made,
My meanings all waylaid,
And all I am lying clear
With no interior,
And my bones sprawled out white
And shining in the Light

Second Deposition

Sometimes I look inside
and see a mountain slope
in Colorado. There
my grief comes trickling down
from the packed snow of my hate
freshly, spring after spring,
through darkness under fir trees.

You've seen such places, maybe.
There breed the little wild trout,
the brooky and the cutthroat
in their icy brilliant colors,
there, under branches sagging
or broken from the snows,
the thin song of mosquitoes
criss-crosses the chill air,
there, tiny colored stars
on the dark of the wet sphagnum,
a few mountain flowers tremble,
fine roots washed in snow water,
the colors clear and cold
—almost too small to notice
should you stray under there,
certainly too small to pick.

And These

And These

Out of an occasional delight
in those icy vacancies
that stretch away
from the 'comforting stench
of comrades'
            mostly
of a simple, bi-partite
structure like the fungus
living with an alga
to make a lichen, some
2,000 species of which
inhabit the Arctic, fastened
to rocks, pieces of bone,
cast-off antlers, so cold
and barren and dark
their situation, some of them
may grow only during one
day in a year—in the long
darkness each bright patch
holding fast to its object.

Five O'Clock

Just before hitting the turn
and entering the down ramp
hunched up and tensed again
and the little new moon in the west
by herself in the early darkness
cocked backward so jauntily
on the steep downward slope
into the wintry ocean

Dec. 19, 1975

A malformed and much sophisticated world
it is, and I in my fiftieth winter of it
with a few ordinary things known, matters of doing,
matters of desire, and there's the full moon
in the workshop window again,
with its old silent abruptness, light
held cleanly inside its firm rim,
lifting so clear and cold
over the wintering poplars—scrawny
columns of brush upfountaining
through how many years? over
the worn and frozen lawn, grove
and grass burning white together

The Study Window

All tired out in the morning,
yeah, and the moon there, old
in the midmorning sky, white
and worn away on one side
so thin, the sky shows through,
in the stillness above the crisp
snow peaks of the winter mountains.

March 16, 1976

Home for the convalescence, stepping
Out on the patio, the sun
Shining at full strength on me,
And there, aslant in the shadow,
Is our young maple, that had been
A forked stick all winter,
With its new leaves, each pale,
Just uncrimping from the confinement
Of its bud, individually distinct
At the tips of the thin twigs—
Dark, overlapping, they will make
Heavy clumps in the summer and be
The main fact of the tree, but don't yet
Belong to it, still glistening
In the film of their newness, out in the air
Like a scatter of little green birds,
The pointed lobes of the leaves
With the shape and tilt of wings.

The Window: in Time of Drought

The camelia leaves against it
will be sleeked with the cold
wet, despite their jouncing
under the big drops
and then the air going
gray green with the rain
clattering suddenly,
water bunched, quivering,
dragged by the heavy wind
in long diagonal welts
across the old window,
as if the glass were melting—
as it is, in fact, the panes
being thicker at the bottom,
ever so slightly,
after all these years, from the slow
downward pour of the glass

A Young Slug on the Counter, by the Wet Wrapper of the Paper

Brought in unawares—suddenly
Airborne as he was clambering
Over the Times in his cruise
Across the rainy sidewalk
In the early November dark.

And now on the move again,
Singlemindedly, belongingly,
In the warm lit kitchen,
His rain-freshened, mucusy skin
Glistening, clean as the porcelain tiles;

And meanwhile, to imagine, still
Travelling through his tissues
Toward the immaculate dark
At his center, the phosphorus-cold glow
Of his wonder: shy, by itself, slow.

Soliloquy

Home as are his brothers on a visit
and now saying as we sit at dinner
'After dark I walked out from camp
under the pine trees and wondered
where the light was coming from,
there was no moon. I looked up
and it was stars, I've never seen
so many big stars so close together,
and right over me was Orion,
with his legs down in the branches.
The sky had more light area than dark;
And in the trees, stars were shining
in the smallest openings.'

The Ross's Gull

Whenever the Arctic winter nears
and the white sun just clears
the earth's rim and the tundra colors go
under the new snow
and the terns and plovers make their flight
away from a solid night
and ptarmigan, fox, owl, hare
turning white, disappear
on the white space under the black
and the gulls, too, fly
by coast and open waters down
to where there's green and brown,
the Slaty-backed, the Glaucous, the pale
gray Iceland gull—
then the little Ross's gull makes a strange
migration from his summer range
in north Siberia—heading northeast;
most lovely and known least
of gulls; his plumage a delicate rose. . . .
northeast then north he goes
beyond Point Hope, and Icy Cape, and past
Point Barrow till at last
he disappears, with his graceful, wavering flight
into the polar night
and his cry *a-wo a-wo a-wo*
kiaw! drifting back slow.
There he will fly and sleep and eat

for some nine months in the complete
darkness—God's own darkness, surely—
over the Arctic sea,
feeding among the open water cracks
in the shifting polar packs
(so the authorities suppose,
nobody knows)
in his fresh rose feathers no one can see
up there, not even he.

"graceful, wavering flight," and most of the information, are
borrowed from Arthur Cleveland Bent's Life Histories of
North American Birds, Gulls and Terns.

In the Canyon

More distinct
than ever we

can be,
their ways

remotely
crisscrossing ours,

gods
each

with his one
virtue

(or maybe two
or three)

by itself
simple,

disclosed
with such unintended

sureness and
so glancingly

passing across
the eye piece

of our
complicated and

clumsily aimed
attention

—of birds the big flicker
his cry from a treetop clanging
in the first light: how to begin.
And the deer, for the body's lightness, surprised
at mid-day, russet and a hint of antlers
over the green bushes then gone,
as if he had not been in motion but hanging there
when the whole forest shifted a little
and concealed him—
the bear for knowledge
in detail—there is no other—of his terrain, and
for his unhurried gait
that takes him so rapidly
where he wants to go, his company
his solitariness—and for his capacious
robe of sleep for the long cold and darkness,
and in the new grass by the footpath out back
the green and yellow striped
garter snake that shows every time
how innocence startles,
the snail for his hush,
the grasshopper, of insects, for alertness
and his lucky look

Spring

We two at our reading this evening
making a busy stillness in the room
when the singing of a mockingbird
came fresh and loud
straight into my ear
from the long empty, black
cave-mouth of—the cold dark lung
of the fireplace, beside my chair.

End of September

However it may be with me
Lying wakeful in the old bed
This night is cool, fresh, quiet,
Moon blanched, a few late season crickets
Trill under the oaks across the road,
Some of the moonlight, coming through
The pine tree by the window,
Burns like lumps of phosphorus, on the bedclothes.

Reader Listening

Rain now with dark coming on
after the chill clear day, and it makes
coming against the roof a roof of sound.
Many mild little comments,
with the occasional loud drop,
the faint ones, the pitch
differences, the many drops striking
at almost the same time, the
individual sounds still audible
in the general run of sound as the rain
comes down heavier, loudening
on the roof, the sense of this change
belonging with the sense that comes
when an animal one has been watching—
say a bear, soaking himself in a creek—
suddenly & calmly changes position—
when on the window ledge
a series of drops begins falling,
starting up an excited little
local tempo, and then, oddly, slows down
and at last stops while the heavy rain
continues

. . . and leaving, then,
for that first companion
of your mere existence (before
you established relations even
with yourself, or your human mother)
the immense brood-beast
the natural universe, where
for instance Homer's 'dark earth
and starry sky and strong-running ocean'
are a corpuscle eddying—
                              not
to be home any more,
with a consciousness like the house
built joist and stud and rafter
in time, in human lengths, not
to pause even at the nestling
of chemical to chemical,
but entering those subtle barrens
where billionths of seconds go,
under the whole show
(leptosome to the last!),
into the sheer and clear
orderliness of chance
where the numbers do their dance
of no location—haunt,
if what I've read is so,
of Heisenberg, and Planck,
and the quiet magister, Gauss

Third Deposition

The lamp throws a pleasant warmth
on the back of the hand, its soft white light
floods shoulder fingers pencil note pad
and desk surface, notes on old soiled scraps of paper,
The Hölderlin, the glasses case, the black bowl
by Blue Corn, the Hokusai Fishermen Draw in their
    Nets
While a Poet Meditates in a Distant Hut
cut out of an old Time, years ago,
the Porsche ad, The City Porsche, a blue-silver
914 driven by a blonde up a hill in San Francisco
the 0.5 liter earthenware coffee mug,
the drafts of a poem, "migraine's fancy
stitching" a phrase at the corner of the eye,
piles of old letters—the latest from Helle—
a lucite box of dry flies, clippings of reviews
of books wanted, a lump of turquoise and
a piece of white granite veined with green
from the Snowy Range in Wyoming,
white glue, a pen light disassembled
its batteries exposed, a bit of paper folded so
that a quote from Pope sits up, and crawling across
all this comes the black cat, Christmas, so much
admired by the family, cautiously lowering
and lengthening her body, one glossy paw
testing for a spot to sleep in, she finding
it really is hopeless here, settling instead
for the window shelf, hind quarters on a New York
    Review
front quarters, and cheek, on an old rabbit pelt,
a paw curled over her eyes.

53

Toad Sweat

τεττιγα δ'εδραξω πτερον

Fragment

         . . . Self
the sly continuator; peevish; writhing
knot of flat-eyed appetites,

no one of which ever notices
the others it's tangled with; old

shapelessness, incessantly bringing on
disorderly assemblies of shapes;

busy attractor of swarms
of gnat-miseries with its sweat; deep

well of pity for its own plights
and tireless accumulator of grievances; inflamed

and swollen with the merit
so gained, with gleeful resentment

concealing its own indestructible
talent for moderate happiness; constantly

aching to be changed into now this
now that icon of calm felicity

Father and Child

These are the case-hardened fingers
With which I bring to your pink
And drooling mouth your food
From farther away than you think
        But sleep,
Sleep in the natural dark.

With this electronic sound
I shall teach you what to do,
My son, as I now sing
Lullaby for love of you.
        Now sleep,
Sleep in the natural dark.

Fetched from the polymerized
Thermoplastic womb,
Now blue-eyed and golden-haired
And shapely and firm of limb!
        Sleep, sleep,
Sleep in the natural dark!

Under this coat spun of cooled
Chemicals is the shoulder of chrome
That will edge you after a while
Out of your gleaming home
        (Now sleep,
Sleep in the natural dark)

Whereupon you will ascend
Chock full of your own desires
On your own titanium wings

Driven by chemical fires,
        But sleep, now,
Sleep in the natural dark,

The night wind and a bough tip
Brushing the pane make a mild,
Serious, purposeless music,
O my strange human child.
        Sleep, now,
Sleep in the natural dark.

Meeting Old Mr. Jim Porcupine

At the reading—somewhat country-boy,
it's just you people and me, here;
open, simple, sincere—mind you,
clever enough never to be
anything like *them*. There are certain ideas
none of us would be caught dead with, which makes
our being here together—well, pleasing.

The trouble is, I remember
how very savvy, how cagily nice
and quick on his feet the fellow was
when he stopped by to visit earlier,
though I still sat there supposing it was just conversation
till after a while I began to feel in my skin
the fine little needles of—what's this, malice?

Friends, imagine seeing out in the woods
your ordinary old lumbering porcupine
and he commences capering around you
with, by God, the smooth quickness
of a monkey, and while you stand there gaping
he's busily firing his quills into you!
I know, porcupines don't do that.

But your canny, enterprising sentimentalist does.

The Career

By means long since too commonplace to mention
(Taught, therefore, in the classrooms of the land,
With diagrams) he captured their attention.
How anxiously they came to see him stand
With a loop of his intestines in each hand!
      He was no Indian giver.
He fed them with his two lungs and his liver.
His call was 'Come and see a man unmanned.'
He diced his heart and kidneys. He became
      All mouthed name,
     And then they took the blame.

Winter Child

Never mind now, I am delighted,
my happiness is complete—
the individual human now recedes
with his motley moderations
on moderate little earth
these days of October,
November, December, when
the mother darkness and cold
come back and the father light
wheels low, aslant, unconcernedly
withdrawn into remoteness,
in the extravagance
he blazes with, and we
come back into the mineral
sleep (a little way) from which
rousing so keenly
in the cold
we see and hear nothing
but the Heart's red fires in the dark, in
the end Silences
where reign the archaic King
and his Queen, that was
before him, in the Beginning.

———

In the Habitat of
the Magpie

Oh we will get out of here
Where everything's impure, not clear,
Where, as they say, it's all shades of gray,
Won't we, old self (though time I fear
Is getting on . . .) —like the magpie
We saw springing up today
Lightly from his putrid, smeared meal
On the pavement, his feathers
Such a fresh black and white.

The Accident

"A poem does not come into existence by accident."
> —*Professors W. and B. on the way to discovering
> the Intentional Fallacy.*

Dear Mother Muse,
> We *thought*

we were being careful.
But it appears to be
a very healthy little poem.

Near the Stairs

This busy lame-brain,
This picker-up of ideas
Discarded by their owners,
This maimed intelligence
Hobbling to catch up,
Eager to compete, arriving
At the arena after
It has emptied, this
Challenger and flincher
With the wrecked, zestful mentality,
This poor devil, pity
And keep clear of him,
He'd trip you with his crutch
Should he find himself beside you
At the head of the stairs.

Fragment

. . . and still, deep down, in your personal
La Brea Tar Pits, sunken
some of them these twenty years,
like so many mastodons, sloths,
sabre-toothed tigers,
this hulking collection
of old hatreds, perfectly preserved.

Running at Hendry's

For head with foot hath private amitie
And both with moon and tides.

Note

I've always loved the old sonnet sequences more than
any of the sonnets in them, magnificent or lovely as these
may be. The sequences take up as no single
poem can the unpredictable mix of experiences and
themes with the prevailing passion, all going on during a
longish stretch of time. Then there are the scraps of
narrative that come out incidentally, the shifts (alas) in
the passion itself, the sense that each poem is being done
at a sitting with the time passing, that an idea that
doesn't come through satisfactorily here may turn up
later (only now with a fresh secondary theme jostling it
which later becomes itself a main theme), the untidy
couplings of metaphysics and peevishness, jealousy or
other unworthy emotions, this or that unrelated
preoccupation obtruding along the way, the speaker
himself changing willy-nilly, the bits of news, glooms,
dull stretches, elations—and the old types, the
anniversary sonnet, the insomniac sonnet, the sonnet
about the sonnet.

When I found myself taking up running
at the height of the craze, a byproduct was that phrases
kept coming to mind, pieces of poems, having to do not
only with running but also with the not especially
beautiful or otherwise remarkable beach where I ran. I
had come to love the place for its shapes, tones, smells
and the rest, not least the people that showed up there.
All this, with its daily, hourly changeableness, I was each
day looking forward obsessively to visiting. So here was a
passion, and it occurred to me that I could cross the new
craze with an old craze and do a sonnet sequence,

drawing on whatever came in handy in the older craze, for treatment of what I was doing down at Hendry's nearly every day, over the weeks, the months, the unspectacular seasons.

After Work: Foreword

Home, then out of the canyon and inch past
Shopping center, school; inch over freeway;
Veer with the creek that notches the pale clay
Headlands and I am at the place at last.
The shoreline hereabouts runs east and west.
Clear days there's islands to be seen, any day
Sky, sand, waves, light, birds, dogs, people. I'd say
Late in the day in winter is when it's best.
Down the long, slant beach, and the wave-tips catch
The sun's low fire, the wet sand's all red light,
The shorebirds eat red light—and all goes gray
The moment you turn back the other way,
Cliffs, sea, and sky a great cave, in dead light;
And the fresh darkness settling, in the stretch.

Running at Hendry's

1. Down Here after Being Kept Away Three Weeks by Sickness

How much I missed this place. While I've been gone
The season has turned, the winter birds are here,
The sand is firm, clean, smooth, and the air clear
With a wave flashing cold in the low sun
Under the slow wingbeats of a pelican
That three pilfering gulls keep swinging near,
Whimbrels and godwits and plovers and killdeer
Work the sleek shallows, I begin to run:
Easy, now. But I swear the beach gives back
My footthuds like the tightly stretched buckskin
It looks like here, the blazing water track
Of the sun's running beside me—coming in
The old ocean commotion and the dark mass
Of a jogging girl's hair jouncing as we pass.

2. Commotion

Under a low fogbank, the blackish tone
Of its belly darkening the waves and sand
And cliffs that block all view of the high land
Where the town sits in sunlight, I'm alone,
The beach is bare, the hard brown sand slopes down
Steeply to the low tide. From where I stand
No jogger rounds the point to scare the band
Of godwits from their meal. I'll start my run
Together with the dark sea running in
From a horizon turning steely bright
(Sun finishing its run where the fog's thin)
While jaegers and gulls keep up a running fight
Whirling sharp black against that piece of sky
The beach and cliffs run toward and likewise I.

3. Liberté, Fraternité

More fog.—Have you seen a gross, heavy-legged deer?
Or in a flight of terns some with the bill
Twisted and blunt, some with stub wings, some small
As wrens? Imagine an ectomorphic bear.
No, shaped by the shapes of water and earth and air
They move in ruthless grace and crucial skill
Unfree and strong and evenly beautiful,
Unprovided with souls, completely clear and here.
I pass a poor old woman, six feet three,
Mannish, who has a heron's jerky stride,
Just as a well-built fellow passes me.
Next, hairy breasts swinging from side to side,
An obese youth rounds the point; and better weather
Brings many another of us out here together.

4. Beach Litter

Slipped through the fingers of my writing-hand
Already in these dozen days or so—
The grove of winter trees, intaglio
Complete with twigs, carved in the hard smooth sand
(While the waves keep on rushing in to land
In the old uproar) by the trickling backflow,
And running in fog, and the young pair who go
Down beach apart, I see the fellow stand
With his back to her while she with her eyes
Downward walks this way, that way—coming in
I pass and hear her humming cheerfully,
And the cold light one dusk far out at sea
And the time I finished fast as if to win,
Some girl's clear laugh away down the beach the prize:

5.

—Or the man and the old woman seated at either end
Of a long bench that leans and sags rustily:
Though sudden raw weather has cleared the beach, and
   she
Is dressed none too warmly, she keeps with a thin hand
Her jacket collar closed and reads on as she'd planned,
It looks like, in an old paperback, all the while he
Dressed up as for a party—a party refugee?—
Stares, with his elbows on his knees, at the cold sand:
Or the leopard seal lying long dead and swollen tight
Getting his spots changed for him, all right, by the sea
And the sea air: or that strong old man in serious
   thought,
Bareheaded, in a workman's clothes—a machinist,
   maybe;
The last runner in, I met him stalking doggedly out
Between dark sea and cliffs in the fast-failing light.

6. The Pelican-watcher (1)

Dusk under fog; and under fog a mist
Grays out the view three hundred yards off shore,
Ocean, though wind's no harder than before,
Smashes and roars where it had slapped and hissed
All week long, beach may be at its ugliest
Heaped up with kelp torn from the ocean floor,
Huge clots and strings of it, yellowy brown, and more
Comes heaving and sprawling in on every crest.
Few birds. It's townsfolk out for the spectacle
And hundreds of surfers: black torsoes holding still
As tree stumps in the troughs, awaiting the right one.
No pelicans. I miss them, on my run.
Then, five of them! infixing their reflection
In the wave's wall they fly along to perfection.

7. The Pelican-watcher (2)

There must have been five hundred here last week
Not grazing the waves like these but swirling high
Their silhouettes jagged against a sky
Bright silver in the west over a sleek
And blazing evening sea; slow, homely, meek
Amongst the agile lovely terns and sly
Gull gangs they flapped deliberately by.
Ungainly dives get them the fish they seek.
They look like so much scrap-iron hurled in the air,
But they belong. Archaic and venerable
Their ugliness no less than their steady skill
(And now alas who's jogging towards me there?
A handsome colleague whose talk is a display
Of intellectual cowardice and decay. . .).

8. Running with my Sons

Two of them home by chance the same weekend!
I fight a fear that's like Ben Jonson's fear,
Of being too glad of having them down here
Running abreast with me on the hard smooth sand.
And all the better it is for being unplanned:
I have no heed for shorebirds, or the clear
Sunlight inside the wavelets rippling near,
Or other runners, or the familiar blend
Of surf- and gull-noise. —One of them sprints away
Spattering through the shallows like a pup,
I say to the other "Don't let me hold you up,"
And off he spurts. I watch them happily.
How they shine! across the difference of years,
And will shine in my day fears and night fears.

9. Running with my Sons

Fifty-one runs with nineteen and twenty-three
Thinking "by hap of happy hap", the phrase
Cast by the crude old Tudor, well displays
The kinship of happiness and luck . . . I see
From the corner of my eye how springily
The boys are striding, how their breathing stays
Easy and light. Not so with them always,
Both once rode crutches after surgery.
We round the second point and they run on
Into the haze, down beach I've never run,
While I turn back, and think of how that stretch
They're running is like the years I'll never reach;
And think helplessly, how will it be for them?
It'll be the same and sharply not the same.

10. More Hap

Bad omen in the morning and once more
Late in the day, encountering face to face
Two sons of bitches, each at a time and place
I'd never seen either one of them before.
And the day, picketed by this polluting pair,
Went wrong, running in the dusk I now retrace
The slight brain-lurches that put me off my pace . . .
The slippages of heed that are my despair!
So I run along full of my latest blunder—
And everything's still, but a distant simmering
From the sea, the light rakes low, the tide is neap,
In the strange peace I nearly halt in wonder
At water in thin clear layers wavering
On the flat sand—a kind of shining sleep.

11. Delights of Winter Evenings Down Here

Saturday night. The ranger's shut the gate.
In the deep dusk I make his figure out
Eyeing me as I wheel the Z about
Five yards from his white gate-bars and hesitate
At the open Exit. Never before so late,
I park on up the road. He has the clout
To turn me back, I half expect his shout
As I slip through the nearly dark parking lot:
Cold wind. Dark sea with sharp little peaks all over.
This long bright strip I'm running on is lighter
Than the sky! Back where the beach is dark some water
Or foam—no, the white patch on a wing is flashing.
Five terns—still seeing fish!—plunge, wheel, hover.
Black stubs of surfers lift on a swell—*that's* passion.

12. God-light

Low dark cloud-cover and ocean make a pair
Of jaws held just apart; in the opening,
Where I now run, no room for anything
But the cliffs, now bleakly pale where they are bare.
At the horizon, a low, cold light just where
The sun has set; I watch it briefly cling
At the sea's rim—clear God-light, the real thing—
While I run on through suddenly darkening air.
Under the cliffs are sanderlings and plovers
Busy with their last feeding for the day;
And a few people—a lone girl there, two lovers,
An old lady with her dog; and part way
Down the cliff ahead a house hangs, with a flight
Of stairs down to the beach, and window light.

13. House

Though days may pass and you'll see no one there
The place is lived in always. There was the sight
You could have seen in clear, still evening light,
Of a girl trimming a bearded young man's hair
Out on the littered deck, and you might hear
The little dog's wow-*wow*! when running late
And alone below, for months a drying skate
Swung under the deck, wetsuits and suchlike gear
Hang from the railings. Looks like a fine life.
Sometimes one of them waves as they come and go
Casually in view of us passersby below,
While they hang half in the air on the steep clay;
That the house is going, waves chewing away,
Is habit-knowledge with them, as between man and wife.

*A big storm struck shortly after this was written, some of the
cliff gave way, and one of the family was interviewed in the
paper: "I know what it's like to live with the sound of
concrete popping, but when you love to live here. . . ."*

14. Running Late

Last class goes overtime, there's some delay
Getting an ace bandage on an aching knee
At the right tension, and then hurriedly
Into slow, slow traffic: the last light of day
Fades off the clouds above my getaway,
Though there at last and running I can see
The sickle moon reflected, glittery,
Like a surf-perch, in a wave; under the play
Of water sliding in and sliding back,
This sand is a seal's flank, the inch high hiss
Of that foam edging, somehow throws a black
Shadow in this faint light; my emphasis
Was haste-blurred on those lines of Herbert's. How
I'd like to have the class back (briefly!) now.

15. Running Late, Having Held the Class on Herbert Overtime to Look at Three Lines

Deep dusk, the quarter moon strong enough now
To show in the wave's flank with a fish-like glitter,
I run on the dark beach thinking, This is better
Than the delicate orange clouds two days ago
In pale green sky, too pretty. (Are there no
Other runners here for once?) Thinking, That wetter
Sand there shines like some membrane, this twitter
Of sleepy sanderlings says it must be so
That I'm the last one out, that subdued roar
Of water's a not-word I have heard before,
And suddenly there comes the one thing more
I ought to have told the class, that not elsewhere
In English is that thought thought—and see how clear
And passionate and quiet it is there.

16. Running against a Cold Wind

A bleakness about the place, with the wind keen,
Dark ocean under it running like a full
Rough icy river. A bright diagonal
Of orange cloud slopes over the whole scene.
The sky below it's turning that strange pale green
Coleridge in his dejection couldn't feel
The beauty of. I think of the tall girl
Who glanced my way as I came driving in,
And again later as I began my run
And passed her with her friends, and how her presence
Filled for a time the whole place like a fragrance.
Hard going now! lungs hurting, and she long gone
And everyone else but me, the whole scene stark,
Even the cliff house windows staying dark.

17. And the Fat One Gripping a Bottle of Wine

Blazing November. The wrongness of this weather's
   what
Makes my being here for anything all wrong, the sea
Having gone slack and pale and bland and summery,
The air since the first light this morning dry and hot
And motionless. Broad day's brought everybody out.
There goes a runner threading through a family
Straggling along in street-clothes. Surfers unseeingly
Step around three elderly ladies. All tramp my holy spot.
I run on sand where multitudes lay and strolled and sat.
It's scuffed and stale. And heading back through the
   overused scene,
Around the last point I see alone out on the flat,
Where the sand's newly wet, one fat girl and one lean
Briefly link arms and dance, whirling this way and that
Over their clear, prancing reflections in the sheen.

18. Running with a Poem from the Latest TLS in my Head

A hot breath off the land at my turnback spot.
A streak of skunk-scent a little further down.
Sea quiet in the late dusk. No moon
As yet. The hard sand uneven underfoot,
Much trampled on. An airliner's headlight
Makes a big white star in the orange coming on
In thin clouds fanning out from the set sun—
Orange, and a real green, staying clear and bright!
But what I think of's the Britisher with the dripping
    nose
Who thinks we'll think he's tough because he says
Evil is tough and sure of itself and Good
Is gentle, irresolute. You know how it goes?
St. Thomas More, for instance, living in a daze?
Samuel Johnson, so lacking in hardihood?

19. Moon Measuring

Moon'll be rising. There's a few people here
In the chill of the sundown, some of them regulars—
Old tilt-hat's there on his bench, photographers
Stand waiting for the colors to appear
As the sun drops. Pelicans swing in near
The flat beach where the sea now mildly stirs.
They fly in line, casting a row of blurs
Of pelicans on the slick swells they barely clear. . . .
The boys are home, all three of them this time.
But they ran earlier. Turning back I pause
To watch the dead white half moon on its climb,
Which one of them said, a lunar month ago,
"Looks like a helmet" as he rejoined his slow
Parent along this stretch. And so it does.

20. Sonnet in Printer's Greek

Than sky or water. freenn tthom her hands,
How can they see? Bylypsoorr else a lover. . . .
Mallards float in the color. Llcck stobs hover.
Msidli advationfir ent shining bands.
A liitle bleak. yllongg undulant ands.
Smell off slifftop, excloomong. Woll uncover
Not much rmmm. And veers abruptly out over
Face tense. Breathing iv arq demands.
Or flash of foam. Blicypp, old sonneteer . . .
Abwarss in hero telic imperfection
Whyever not, Considerink the clear
Though sanderlings ssyvrrr which one's direction
Swer.kho in concert almost disappear.
Abdi nec dog runs on the red reflection.

21. Death Song

Not the dead seal swollen tight as a football
That I saw, clear in the midday winter light,
But my students at their final exams last night
Was my death vision. And no, not Nancy's skull
Under her smooth skin. I saw death edge them all
As they toiled there, it rested at the white
Surface of papers I had, curved with the tight
Curve of the c in precise, kept the interval
Between each letter (and gives this cold salt air
Its underlightness, the moon its bright rim because
Death is what does not happen, around what does),
I held in my lungs its imperishable elsewhere,
I saw creation being supported by
Death's tortoise—not on his shell, in his air-clear eye.

22. Visitation

No running is the doctor's order. Glumly enough
To walk along and watch the other runners run,
And the sky fires up smoky crimson, and the sun
Slips into a sea suddenly darkening and rough
Out from the shore. Tide's out. Where the sand levels off
And where I like to go, the water's coming on
In terraces, shining layers, the nearest one
So thin it is a skin of light to trudge and scuff
And watch the slowly deepening color on, until
There is my holy of holies: a sandy-floored recess
Under the cliffs, half hidden behind a rock outcrop.
Always when I am running this is where I stop
And turn back. What now? Careful! A brief pause, I
    guess,
With the merest sidelong glance will do or nothing will.

*It was a Greek mistake to connect the sacred with the
permanent, the sacred being phenomenal like everything else,
and the transient conjunction of chance and those necessities
whose most apt expression is mathematical. Three weeks after
this poem was done, the holy place was destroyed by the
combination of a high winter tide and huge waves that
changed the shapes of the cliff-bases and heaped storm-
wreckage—much of it freshly splintered trees—high up
against them.*

23. Colleague with a Notebook

Beach wide and flat. I run, dully, on a sheet
Of neutral-colored light, slipping along
In the wet is a blurry quarter moon, a tongue
Of water pushes in quietly over the wet,
Quick-sliding, low-hissing, its tip of foamy white
Entering up the sand. Then I'm among
The seal brown, seal high rocks—old seals and young
Seaward they slant, alertly—exposed of late
By the winter tides . . . slowly, on the way back,
Darkness coming, the horizon turns a bright,
Deep orange-red, the exact color of the throat
Of a cutthroat trout! Pass a man writing a note
(His camera's set up) and look back—beach black
Where he stands, crossed with great slashes of light.

24. Loiterer

But the water—a half inch deep there, sidling in,
Rumpling to sharp little ridges, with elegant
Black shadows, in the level light . . . ripplings sent
At an angle through other ripplings cross-hatch, then
The surface quiets, and, smooth once again,
Shivers all over . . . two tiny waves, blent
Head-on emerge, each going the way it went. . . .
New water foams in, slides back clear and thin:
The lovely loiterings, with darkness coming on,
Stay with me as I finish up my run,
Having had to hurry all I did today.
And nothing done well, getting it all done.
"That most exciting perversion," said Hemingway,
Of such forced haste; the feelings fray and splay.

25. The Big Wave

(To Michael Ridland)

Others are leaving as I pull in tonight
Dressed for the chill, and under a dull sky
Gray surf from winter storms is lifting high
Far out from shore, then bouncing in loud and white,
But a kid in trunks straightens to his full height
By his old VW, powerful and—hell, I see
He is one-legged. Now he vigorously
Swings by on his crutches in the failing light.
When I look next he has got off alone
—Christ, to do what? 'Way down the beach, he's thrown
The crutches down and is hopping, his one thigh
In the boiling white, toward a wave three times as high
As he. Hesitates, though. That wave comes on
And he hops back. In the sad, bad light I start my run.

26. Running in America

Saint Kenneth Cooper, with your stethoscope
Stopwatch and clipboard, how they run for you!
Eager and obedient in every thew
Having had courses now on How to Cope
With Death, on how to eat, to screw, to ope-
n doors, breathe, spit, work zippers . . . they can do
The running but you make it all come true
In charts, with points, paying off Faith and Hope:
Dad in his old sweat suit, running head down
Doggedly in the dusk, the stern beauty with the frown,
The young couple goose-stepping *shoulder*-high,
Eyes straight ahead, to warm up—none of them smiles.
I've heard at parties the questions . . . "How many
     miles . . . ?"
And the really serious runner's shy reply.

*At the New School for Social Research you can take not only
"Coping with Death" but "The Philosophy and Psychology of
Death." "We were early in death studies," says the New
School's proud president, John R. Everett.*

27. Light Like the Beautiful Trout Fly Name: Pale Evening Dun

Cold spatter of rain, then wind. Last night the tide
Covering the beach and sliding up the rocks
Along the cliffs, driving the sanderling flocks
And me elsewhere, now a beach five yards wide
All kelp-heaps and scattered stones, and a rock-slide
At the point, wet shale in jagged blocks
Angled for twists, foot-slitherings, bone-shocks;
And pooled and trickling water on every side.
I rock-hop past the next point. Here the air
Is quiet, the ocean crump-crumping its tons
Well out from shore, the nearby water still. . . .
Stretch of smooth sand! with a boulder here and there,
Standing alone—black rock, gray water, duns
Of wet sand, cloud-roofed, in the even light; so beautiful.

28. Running in the Rain, High Tide

Rain slanting past and no place here to run.
In the cold deepening dusk there comes the roar
Of water much too near: as the car door
Caught by a gust swings wide, I see the brown
Waves smack the cliffs. Well, head for the next beach
    down.
Bulldozers have gouged it up and gullies pour
With the runoff, crumbling, forcing me to detour
Through garbage to the blacktop (it's near town).
I run in a dazzle of streetlights and car lights
My glasses streaming, and splattering along
Alone, think of the swaggering word invictus;
And sprint back through the drench against a strong
Headwind, wearing as the car comes into sight
A combination grin and runner's rictus.

29. Christmas Down at the Mission

Tonight sun moon and earth line up and drag
The sea far back, the still tide-pools, like light
Solidified, mirror that great headlight,
The low sun, beaming on. . . but here's the snag:
Been reading in the latest lit'ry rag
From Britain, and in this one doing right
(As with the Pauper Witch) is their delight
In tight-lipped 'leaders'. Made my spirits flag.
I know it's for your own good when they say
"Sit down, my friend, this chilling Christmas day,
Though the bench is hard, the table bare of trimmings,
Hold out your bowl and heed our bracing hymnings!"
Meat gray and stringy, gravy gray and thin,
Served up by the clammy enemies of literary sin.

30. Freezing

I pick my way through a parking lot nearly full
As a miscellaneous, chilly crowd straggles in.
The sea is pale, a barely fluttering skin
Of light, and everywhere, an uncomfortable
Clearness and separateness to things, they have all
Hardened in this sharp air, and I begin
My run bleakly, not much helped out when
A new girl jogger flashes me a smile
For my weak smile; much less when I look off
From the stones underfoot to where there glows
The sun, low now and like a blurred red rose
In its cold cloud. The cold moon clears the bluff,
Full, and almost too bright to look into.
I head home running moonlit through and through.

31. Running in the Early January Cold

The near water heaves bright gray, then deepening
Outward to a dark horizon line as keen
And aloof as the evenly moving, clean
Crest of a wave, or the edge of a gull's wing:
That pale sunset out there hasn't anything
To do with me, with its cloud whorl, its icy green;
There's nothing in the few people I've seen
To catch the eye, and take away the sting
Of the raw cold look of things; and thinking I run
Upright and briskly, I see my shadow: a tall
Pinhead aslant on stilts, going at a crawl
Along the sand; and in that room today
The neutral silence, I feeling in all I say
The desolateness of what's barely begun.

32. The House that Cliff-hangs

Sometimes my run down here's like putting on
Music and after a while not listening.
I tell myself I spot every least thing
As the same, or changed, around me as I run,
And now I see, as the last third of the sun
At the horizon lays a glistening
Road to the house and reddens the west wing,
That the cliff has fallen away. The deck is gone.
There's a piece of railing stopping in mid-air
Above the expanse of raw vertical clay,
Loose dirt, iceplant, and planking sprawled down here,
Storm-loosened—not today or yesterday.
Coming back by in the late dusk I see
The bearded young man contemplating me
      Or else the wreckage there,
      Through the salt atmosphere,
Straight down, from his high, narrow balcony.

33. Willets under an Overcast

This new and winter term is a stopped wheel
To push against, it budges and rolls back
Into its rut in a hard-frozen track
Through the inside country where I think and feel:
Outside the willets land for their evening meal,
Their lifted wings exposing elegant black
And white zigzags, beside the tidal slack:
Gray clouds, gray ocean, and the light still and pale.
Whatever was missing from what I did today
Is the second overcast to run under here,
I puzzle and puzzle under it all the way
To my turn-back place—willets again, a pair
Alight on a black rock offshore, crying *kerlear*!
Teetering prettily, above the sloshing gray.

34. The Nympholept

The crimson sun slipping down through the haze
Smoothly as I arrived is now half gone,
Its color riding the backwash; and I run
And sketch a plan to draw out of her daze
Of shyness Pam who writes so well and faze
The Marxist glibnesses maybe of Juan,
When the girl walks by, barefoot, putting down
Footprints still clear under the water glaze.
Later, it's two girls writing in notebooks
As I come in, in the deep dusk they lean
To see their words. Then still another looks
My way as I get in my car, to say
"Yer a good runner!" I, startled: "Nah."—"I've seen
You often . . . ." drifts through the gloom as she goes
     her way.

35. The Bare Winter Beach

No kites, no frisbees. No baking half the day
Beside her friend, a radio in between.
No babies. Not a six-pack to be seen,
Even gulls are scarce (no garbage). Far away,
Is the big brown belly July puts on display.
—Two lovers, and one walker, dark and lean,
And two runners, are strung out on the clean
Smooth beach ahead, with the light a misty gray
Coming from nowhere and everywhere alike.
A good place for a passion to be worked out
Or up. Near here last night my young friend Mike
Whose wife left him and took their child, did not
See me run by, his eyes so fixed on a pair
Of beauties running by with streaming hair
(Eyes that have been in training on Vermeer).

36. Running with Another TLS Poem in my Head

The bulge of the sea above the benches shows
High tide, and I'll be driven off the sand
Onto the rocks. I should have calmly planned
My run, by the tide-chart, but old drip-nose
Reading his Homer troubled my repose,
Reading his *Times* indeed almost unmanned
Me with his questions. He can't understand
Why gods and heroes cause so many woes.
Odysseus, with his lies and murders—not a bit nice!
Couldn't he practise a gentler kind of vice?
These Afghans, skinning the Russian infidel
Alive! Blood-smeared old Faiths, awake and well,
Inflicting on us still their gruesome folly . . . .
Why can't we all be good, and kind, and jolly?

37. Running in the Rain Again; a Swede with Stout Legs

I run and think of running here the night
After the first big rainstorm of the year,
And the tide low, just a few people here,
Wave-watchers, mostly, shapes making upright
Thick ink-strokes on the louring watery light
Between gray waves and low clouds, and the air
Sharp and the beach vast, gaunt (with here and there
Rank kelp-heaps), bending flatly out of sight.
I'd finished fast and started cooling out,
There's a big Swede nearby doing same,
Stretching and bending and then gazing about—
And edging my way, I see, as if by aim;
He says, "It's beautiful, in its own way,"
Walking past. "Yeh, it's beautiful," I say.

38. Running

Driving down with KABC Sports-talk on,
Author of *The Complete Runner* is the guest,
"How should you breathe?" he's asked, "What is the
   best
Surface for running?" "Is the backbone jarred when you
   run?" . . .
Now that the days are longer, now that the sun
Is up where it blinds me when I'm running west
And the plovers are leaving, all too soon the rest
Of the signs of winter down here will be gone.
Still, Dad in his old sweatsuit and salt-caked shoes
Sends me a wave this time, abrupt and shy,
Without turning his head, and others smile
As *they* pass, and now my mind cuts out, while
In that sudden sort of silence that ensues
When an engine stops, the cliffs blur by . . . .

39. Big Waves in Wind and Clear Cold Sunlight, and the Intelligent New Secretary from the Main Office

Clear from the entrance I could see the spray
Glistening above the cartops like the snow
That banners off the drifts in a big blow,
And once I'm running I watch the falling away
Of waves heaved house-high, and the steady play
Of the cold light on wave-slopes bursting snow
Over the snowy rush and crush below—
Too much for surfers: wave-watchers here today.
And up the beach, a girl sitting quietly
On a big rock, with those waves roaring in.
And it is Marilyn, I recognize
As I come near; sun lights her gold hair pin,
And I start wondering if her blue eyes
Are seeing more than the rest of us down here see.

40. Old Rocks Out in the Late Light

Chill air and the sea sunk, like a lake
In drought-time, back from the gray sand,
A bright place the size of a man's hand
On the waves, where the light comes through a break
In low clouds. And the striped rocks. They take
The eye between flat sea and land,
Humped, leaning, pale band by dark band,
Green bearded, dripping, with pools that quake
In the raw breeze. Here's one pokes out
At our cliffs a heavy upper jaw
That with the lower grips in its maw
The sand I cross. Surely the brief light
Is holy, and holy the darkness light
Makes when it goes, but not that snout.

41. A Quiet Fourth

Homesick, building a fly rod on the patio
All the fresh sunny breezy morning; a calm blue
Sky and green leaves close me in. Low tide's at two,
And I'll run then. —The dusty parade and rodeo
Took place in town, all right, forty-five years ago,
A thousand miles away; fireworks afterwards, too,
And then the ride home on the dirt road, winding
   through
The cool fields in darkness, hearing the water flow
Over the weirs; and then our dogs, at the driveway turn.
—And winter's the time for Hendry's Beach; therefore
   I'll write
This one, to do for my few summer runs down here:
Beach flat, trampled, sea flat, slack and warm and clear;
People little black figures against the big silver light;
Close up, it's beer can, frisbee, radio, sunburn.
                  —July 4, 1978

42. A Quiet Fourth

Fran and I much alone this bright mild day
With the boys scattered, friends too, mostly, so
It's Sousa and Ives out on the patio
(And how subtly the Ives lets the attention stray);
Then work on a fly rod, later get away
For a run at Hendry's, when the tide is low.
My last run down there was six weeks ago—
Summer crowds, and a new fee I won't pay.
But on the Fourth you want a crowd, I learn,
So down I go: beach flat, sea calm, clear, warm.
In and beside it, in every tint, size, form,
People, with frisbee, radio, sunburn.
—Drive back, see centered formally on a top stair
A beer, beneath a flag limp in the cooling air.

$$\qquad\qquad\qquad\qquad\qquad\text{—July 4, 1978}$$

43. The Other Runner
(Recalling, during a
drought, a rainy day
last year)

Wind spread the rain across the glass, I hearing it
While reading Milton all day long, and looking up
From time to time, to wonder when it would stop,
And then forgetting rain, in the warm room where I sat.
Then arriving at the beach: yellow-brown breakers lit
From under a slowly lifting ledge of cloud—the tops
Catching the level blaze, and darkness soon to drop,
And for my run the sand wave-beaten hard and flat.
I ran alone, leaving some saunterers behind,
Beside a set of fresh footprints so far apart
I couldn't match them long, and slowed my pace,
  resigned;
Thinking of Milton, no, of every excellence
How it exhilarates us, and humiliates; while at heart
Spotting the tide approach both sets of the footprints.

44. Dog-days I: Rain-running Recalled

Hard wind, rain; I the only one out here.
Wind on my back, rattle of rain on hat,
Hissing of rain on sand, and beyond that
The noise of the big waves; and small and clear
A whimbrel's call in the din as I draw near
A roaring down the cliff and over the flat
Hard beach—an hour-old river I halt at,
My glasses streaming. The world is a bright smear.
Into a gale now, and the ocean sound
Drowned out by the new howling of the air
Around my head, then even louder pounds
The *hough! hough!* of my lungs inside this blur
Of boisterous air, cliffs, water—startled mind
Along for the ride, body with its old kind.
                    —August 11, 1978

45. Dog-days II: Incidentally Recalling a Dying Sea-lion

—Not that its old kind give a damn for it.
For us who live here, the impersonal
Bright quiet gaze of that dying animal
Put rightly the relation of the fit
And unfit both, to that of which we're knit.
And once the indifference is mutual
Shall consciousness here in the individual
Turn with the whole? the light of light be lit?
I know I saw that seal dying his death
Half sunk into the sand, on the sunny shore,
In the tide-wash: with each wave coming in,
The sand sucking him deeper than before,
The water swirling over his head again,
Subsiding, he catching another breath.

46. Anniversary
(Down here to run after a
runless month abroad)

Life's uneventful, and while we were gone
The season turned; the winter birds are here
And the crowds gone, and the salt atmosphere
Is sharper, with a low hazed-over sun
Laying its wide and glittery roadway on
Gray ocean that looks lonely. Like last year.
—Over the cliffs two hang-gliders appear,
Slope in and land nearby; I start my run.
Sand smooth, smooth! for a runner or a flyer
In this gray light and chill air's misty blend
And the sanderlings, lively, lovely, never tire,
And the sun suddenly lights a deep red fire
Up on the sand, using a beer can end,
And all of it makes up my heart's desire.

47. The Partly-written Page

Life's uneventful. What I remember most
At the odd moment or lying wide awake
At three A.M., is not the storms that shake
Oranges from the groves on up the coast
And wash them out to sea (this year some crossed
The bows of fishermen watching gray whales break),
Litter the shore with splintered trees and make
The news: X houses ruined, X lives lost.
What has stayed with me is such a thing as this:
I come in through the late dusk from my run,
A girl at the picnic table glances over
A half a page of writing she's just done,
Then stares out where the dark waves slap and hiss
Under the darker rainy low cloud-cover.

48. Company

There's Giles again, the lanky fellow who,
Working towards a PhD in Greek,
Likes girls (and always runs with one, a sleek
Beauty at that) mirabile dictu.
—But there's one running because she was told to
By Runner's World. And some journalist has the cheek
To call on us to go, seek out the weak
And sick and scorned: we happy running few. . . .
Loneliness is not possible for this
Long distance runner, I spend my mother wit
Dodging the latest book you dare not miss,
This goddamned merchandiser plucks my sleeve,
Holistic priests approach—I bob and weave,
I detour past the bull- and the horseshit.

49. The Rebecca Mae

After the loud storm she lay off shore low
In the water, grating on rocks. Then a huge wave
Beached her and she looked good enough to save,
Engine and all. Half sunk in sand now, though.
All of us eye her as we come and go,
Runners and saunterers. But she never gave
When kids tried prying her from her half grave.
Soon her name's under. Just her gunnels show.
Still the big seas aren't done with her. One day
We find her resurrected, all the way
Past the next point, then later scattered out
Against the cliff, till her last splinter's under
The sand we pad on; now a well-buried boat
To muse on running through the water-thunder.

50. Night-piece

Lying in the long dark, insomniac,
I see it clearly: sea and beach and air
And a red winter sun, down low, for fire
For the fourth element made out by the Greek
On Sicily's coast two dozen centuries back—
Fire that'll turn me into atmosphere
After I'm dead, and ashes tossed out where
Maybe they'll wash ashore. I hear gulls creak,
And put my being in with the elements
We share with the whole show, rather than
With the odd creature in it that is man
Or with my self, still odder . . . till the tense
Weavings of wakefulness begin to fray
Loosen and come apart and float away—

Phrasing in lines 11 and 12 taken from Santayana's
Dialogues in Limbo.

50 continued.

Not bad, for night thoughts, but as Hemingway
Noticed, night thoughts on recollection,
Deep as you went for them, don't pass inspection
Laid out and drying in the light of day.
Something on which there is not much to say,
Sheer Nothingness, once more escapes detection,
Though disciplined minds can reach by indirection
What the imagination hides away. . . .
Yes, *darkness, sundown, water*—take your pick
Of pictures: wings, a little boat, dark blue
Of gentians, you can't make any of it stick.
So human, moving, lovely, and untrue.
By the fresh light of morning being bound
To bony phrasing if not resounding, sound.

51. Sanderlings Here

A low fog bank to run inside today,
Wave noises muffled, near cliffs blurred and pale.
Fog-puffs come down, each spreading a black tail,
A black bill aimed at the sand. And a slight gray
Movement ahead suddenly swerves this way
And a whole flock gleams cleanly purposeful
Against the drifting vapor. Now they all
Vanish up there, sheering themselves away.
And near the finish, a flat stretch, bits of shells
And pebbles lift a little and begin
To travel along the water ahead of me—
Sanderlings, running in the fog or else
Low-gliding, I here running heavily
As faintly they shape unshape and shape again.

52. "Who prop, thou ask'st, in these bad days, my mind?"

Yeh, summer beach, young riders thudding past
Punching out clear hoofprints beside the white
Spill of the waves, against the low sun's light
The black shapes of the horsemen dwindling fast,
And here, attached to each of the sand-crumbs cast
Beside the hoofprints, a little stalactite
Of shadow, while I mope along and fight
The gloom my reading's put me in last. . . .
Cheer up. What if you must throw in your lot
With Gittingses and Thompsons now, and not
Go back to those they've told on for the ages,
Those monsters Hardy and Frost. You'll get, God knows,
A generous friend in Lawrance Thompson's pages,
Largeness of soul¹ in Robert Gittings' prose.

---

¹*Gittings records with approval the verdict of Mr. Clodd that in Hardy "There was no largeness of soul."*

53. Running with the Pollution

I run and coordinating agencies
A panel of experts new measures called for
The decision-making process funding more
Multi-disciplinary activities
Are in my fatty tissues and all these
Are in my liver supervision war
On crime fact-finding panel a hard core
The underlying causes facilities:
Well, that's our social climate and the air
Carries their fumes and particles everywhere
We breathe. But here's one runner that keeps clear
Of *etic structures* and such—I hear the first
Fibers of these, if you come in or near,
Will cause the alveoli in your lungs to burst.

54. Slinking Off

Open the morning paper, what do you see?
Tom L. and Abby W. in full stride,
The splendid young pair running side by side
Their dog loping between them happily
The finishing touch: I wish them well all three
And damn the lurking journalist who eyed
And caught them coming toward him in their pride
And put them here, a soon-yellowing cliché.
Picture one now, with his thin legs, gray hair
And turkey neck and flapping khaki pants
And nylon shell from the discount drug store
Slipping along down here and wondering
If some other poet . . . deepening in advance
His shame at doing *so* fashionable a thing.

55. Pelican Halcyon

Low tide of winter, beach shines to the eye
Wide as the sea itself for my late run
And the sea light-streaked and smoothed out to a sun
Red in horizon fog, and already high
A piece of the moon's rim, in the neuter sky.
Quiet. Sun flattens to an oval on
The fogbank; to a glowing bar; then gone.
And in the pallor, one pelican flaps by,
Black on the afterglow; and another, black
Out on the pale sea, silently splashing down
Makes yet another pelican silhouette
With the thrown water; I seeing this all alone,
It happens, with the one sound as I head back
The slip-slap of my feet along the wet.

56. Spell Breaking

That is soon over, others come in view:
Old man in street clothes down for a beach walk,
Three women heading back absorbed in talk,
A guy surf-fishing, the odd runner or two.
And no more pelicans: gulls now skreak and mew,
I scare a willet that flies to a safe rock
Kerleer-ing his hurt feelings, a godwit flock
Reflect in the shine they poke their long bills through.
And here's my old friend Herb, facing the sea,
Musing, quite motionless, holding, curiously,
A folded newspaper level with his waist:
Day-offering to sea and sundown, he the priest.
I can't not greet him though the spell will break,
He jogs on in with me for old and new time's sake.

57. Coming Down to Run in Dark and Fog

In the near dark two runners stagger in
Out of the coiling fog along the shore.
Another lurches in, and then two more.
But nobody else here after I begin.
Once I am startled, when the fog-swirls thin,
By a movement I glimpse behind me on the shore.
That's the moon's hard reflection. Airliner's roar
Joins wave-roar for one huge roar coming in
Straight after me; and then a hooded form
Comes by with darkness where the face should show;
It's a runner, though. Small light, with sea below
Is the cliff-house, fog-faint, the one a storm
Last year brought down in part, to crash and splinter,
What's left now pushing into one more winter.

58. Heron Out There

The first cold day of winter, darkness near,
A stiff wind coming in and a high tide
Roaring inshore and everyone else inside
Or heading there, what am I doing here
Plugging through mushy sand, with a wind tear
In either eye, up a beach three feet wide. . . .
Chased by a rush of water up the side
Of the shale at the first point, I slog from there
To the furthest—and the heron I know by day
Is a slab of the dark rock, breaking away
To pass me in the dusk. Down beach again
I spot his still shape—leaf with a long stem.
When I come near he flaps unhurriedly,
Belongingly, into the icy spray,
     Then back the other way
     From me, this time to stay
The long night undisturbed, by the loud sea.

59. The Honesty Boys

I run along beside the little wobbly blur
Of the moon on the sleek wet sand (whereas in the sky
It's holding motionless, hatchet-sharp) and have an eye
On the just-after-sundown ocean's crinkling stir
In the beautiful steel-blue light that suddenly appears,
And find myself thinking again about the way
Certain poets are always putting on a display
Of *honesty*—they bring up yours, and of course theirs,
To your face; sometimes slyly, showing how others are
Dishonest—as one of them just lately tried to tell
All of us Hardy was. That didn't turn out well.
However, credit for trying. . . . On with the essay-war
With each name mentioned being a piece of disputed
    terrain,
Or outpost in the latest *honesty* campaign.

60. The Desolation Light

I came down here one dusk and the beach was gone.
The winter tides were easing it out to sea,
Shelving it down and down, when suddenly
A storm came through and scoured it to the stone—
A jumble of stone; and the sky having done
Its damage loosened up, pale vacancy
Between a lot of ragged cloud debris
Scattering fast, foam yellow and waves brown,
The sea, too, loosened and sprawling, sunk so low
That stubs of rock under for months now showed.
Air darkened as if a curtain had been drawn,
And shining as if for meditating on
Was a tidepool that the gray light had filled
To brimming where a simple stillness held.

61. News

RAVAGED BY NATURE, says the local News,
BEACHES ARE DYING—naturally I read on,
How one day these thin margins will be gone
For good, new sand held back by the dams we use
On our best streams while the sea slowly chews
The old away, back to the cliffs and down
To the stones. And nowhere then to run or sun.
Any dark place can say what else you'll lose:
The canyon air that floats the alder leaf,
The light on the creek, and the creek too, will go;
And the ground under, where it had to flow.
Your sons, and the dear woman who is half your life,
And the two eyes you see both with and through
Will go; and your skeleton; and your spirit, too.

62. Heron Shapes at Dusk

I know the heron that's made this beach his own
Between the headlands, slants like a poised spear
Invisible in the driftwood where I peer—
And there he goes now, flapping off alone.
Later his shape breaks out of some gray stone
That the low tides leave bare this time of year,
Then further down, in deeper dusk, lifts clear
Where only a black tangle of kelp had shown.
Then over by the cliffs, in the near dark there,
I see a heron shape become a girl
Hunched with her trouble there on the driftwood,
The shore a place of human bad and good
Not herons now, so stony stark her stare
At the late red fading from a cloud-swirl.

63. Noon Swimmers, Plovers, a Young Heron, a Grebe

People are black on silver this mid-day
Far up the beach, the waves withdrawing show
Light rustling in the grit, the plovers throw
Shadows appearing solider than they,
And the young heron that lives here flaps away
And alights up ahead in the backflow
That glares more silver as it slips below
The nubs of the bright foam, the sunny spray,
While the grebe I come on has been lying dead,
At the water's edge, on his back. His wings are spread
As if in flight. He looks heraldic, too—
Like the scrawny phoenix D. H. Lawrence drew.
But this bird's missing an eye; draggled and sad
Lies here for a little the only self he had.

64. Heron Totem

Up the long beach, a flock of sanderlings
Will swoop past a ridge of ocean roaring near
(Their white chests flashing), tilt and disappear,
Or pelicans line up, dark, heavy things,
And form one body with a dozen wings
Approaching me head-on, or godwits flare
Warm cinnamon wing-linings on the gray air
When they veer off in the big flocks winter brings.
I love them all, and most this homely one:
Color of driftwood, among the bustlers, the wary
Swervers, he leans inquiringly, and waits.
Slow, frail, ungainly, set for the long run,
Silent with hope, by nature solitary,
He picks his spot, stands still, and concentrates.

65. Politics: Reading the Papers

On the first page, review of Brecht by Spender.
Asks the tough question last: how come he
Clammed up about Stalin?—Because, you see,
Brecht could "play games with evil," with no tender
Conscience, for the sake of future good. (I render
The prose down to its shred of meat.) Page three,
It's Solzhenitsyn—getting by memory
His prose and verse, in the gulag. Old non-bender.
And in the *News*, Bukovsky (Vladimir,
I mean): "I don't like certain ideas because
They bring terrible results." *His* prose is clear.
"The most dangerous thing is when you start
To limit your conscience" *for the noble cause.* . . .
Cold dusk, and time to run . . . where's the tide-chart.

66. Sunday Run:
Starting Out

At the water's edge a baby smacks the beach,
Seriously, then casts me a grave look.
A woman wades along reading a book,
Surf tugging at her legs. And the gulls screech,
And a girl makes a staggering run and reach
For a frisbee through a haze of charcoal smoke
Sharp-scented in the cool air, from a nook
Under the cliffs. We brown and burn and bleach.
And the sober sun, half through the afternoon,
Throws iris-leaf shapes, and squarish glares of light
Along the rollers, sends a quick-sliding thread
Of light along a crest, and overhead
Makes on a softball on its climbing flight
In the blue, a tiny daytime quarter moon.

67. In Public:
Liberté, Fraternité

A photographer sets his tripod up and waits
Among various types down here for the sunset;
The unlovely public—whatever it is creates
Us bungles us. . . . And no colors as yet;
The scuffed-up sand shines gray where it is wet.
The place seems idly jostled, by the gazes
And glances of all these folk, their grunts and phrases.
On the bright gray they bulk in silhouette.

*   *   *   *

And home now, out of the salt atmosphere,
With these things written as I pleased I feel
The doubts crowd in (like a real crowd, watching me
Running along down there), each all too real
And undisguisable deformity
Passing in plain view, in the open here.

68. What the Sea Muttered
(With a variation on a
theme of Goya)

You haven't kept the reader busy enough.
I know, I know—it comes of my long affair
With the clear and ordinary; all my care
May fail to hold the intensity in the stuff.
Too many off-rhymes, rhythms strained and rough,
You crash the delicate old barrier
Between octave and sestet. I declare
My shame before the masters. *You sheer off*
From the whole truth: not even writing of
That day you found you'd fallen out of love
With running down here, much less of harder themes.
—The reason sleeps, and monsters shape the dreams
Which are the things we're doing in broad day,
The monstrous half-done. . . . Nolo contendere.

69. What the Wind Hissed

A chill gray day and a wind began to blow:
Where will you get with that plain water style?
Running's a joke that long since has gone stale,
Seascapes were old a century ago.
I like plain words, I always have been slow.
And the names you drop. Milton of course is vile,
And Hemingway! pathetic macho male . . .
And that brute, Robert Frost. I like them, though.
Why Santayana? Surely you want Saussure.
And Rilke's missing. Really I much prefer
Hardy. *He's fading fast.* Herbert? *OK. . . .*
And Homer? *Fine.* My dirty words? *Passé.*
Here, try a Barthes. Somehow it lacks allure,
Such is my hesychastic mood today.

70. Topophilia

Cold dead light, and the beach, from the long rain,
Like a mud-flat under this low cloud-cope; though where
Sun lights the cloud's far edge a pane of clear
Yellow sky joins it to the steady line
Of the horizon; and tiny and black, and fine
In detail, an oil rig sits precisely there
On the skyline, like some miniature
Electronic component, the thin struts showing plain.
And the space out there clear and empty and fine,
Ready for God to fill—like an Inness, a Lane,
Or even a Hopper: and I think of their
Frank and mystical love of light, and plain
Shapes in the great vacancies of air,
And taking comfort in the bare and spare.

*Hopper, to whom the 'mystical' doesn't exactly apply, said,
'What I wanted to do was to paint the sunlight on the side of
a house.' Inness spoke of 'the hidden story of the real.' With
Lane I had especially in mind the wonderful* Owl's Head,
Maine. *—Santayana writes of the 'something in the human
spirit (which is not merely human), something unreclaimed
and akin to the elements,' that is perhaps at work in these
things.*

Running at Sundown and Dark

Well, it's a pretty sunset—sherbet green,
Orange, even some raspberry, streak the sky
From sea horizon to cliffs. Pelicans ply
The offshore reaches and fishing boats careen
On big waves, giving substance to the scene
With their everyday skillful efforts. Meanwhile I,
Pondering a talk that may well go awry,
Run on the tide-zone's particolored sheen:
Mind pawing obsessively at certain unclear
Distinctions. . . . Pass two more runners; lovers, one
    pair;
A lone girl walking slowly back. It's night
When I come in, distinctions still not right,
Past black stumps in the water just off shore—
Surfers, in the dark there, waiting for one more.

Earlier Poems

from Tree Meditation and Others (1970)

*

—suppose the words came in
the way a flight of blackbirds
I once watched entered a tree
in the winter twilight;
finding places for themselves
quickly along the bare branches
they settled into their singing
for the time.

To Fran

Out in the rain all afternoon
hands and neck chilled—
some trouble, anger

and late supper, the rain
smacking and clicking
outside the room

plenty of chablis
our sparse reflections
on the black window glass

where space comes pouring in
all the way in
from between the stars, in past the blacked out moon—

desolately it enters the room
and streams around your shoulders
without harm—how curious—

and enters my grizzled beard
stopping when it arrives
at the skin warmth—

       *   *   *   *   *

it must be we belong in it—at once remotely
and intimately; the way a sheepherder's fire at night
   belongs
in the distance on a desert upland

What I will Think of as the White Dog Truth

I make out the white bulk in the dark—
the dog approaches at a quick pace
and goes by showing no interest in me,
and such is the quiet of the street
I hear the clicking of his toe-nails
on the blacktop, quick, business-like,
even half a block away, the sound
growing fainter very gradually
and already, while I keep an eye
on the wire-thin half rim of light
the moon shows in a sky jagged
with trees along the bottom—
already this encounter, the white bulk passing
in the dark, the diminishing click
of the toenails along the stretch
of silence back there, cannot be forced
not to have been, the lords of creation
themselves will have to submit to
its having been, if they should find it
some day blocking the way of a desire.

Variation from a Theme by Marsden Hartley

Hartley, summer was plainly for you,
    remarker of joined clearnesses, plover noticer,
    savorer of 'infant clams' and campestris, among the
      opulence,
    'the look of bright everlastingness'

But it is not for me, in summer
    it seems there's nothing to do
    but continue what's become obvious, greens
    overlapping soberly, whitening sky,
    stationary August.

An upper rocky field, and the way
    begins to open, a few bright
    stubble stalks leaning among the clods, nearby,
    and red light flickering in the distance, on the blue
      flats
    where they're burning off the cat-tails in the sloughs,

And 'shall the cold flowing waters
    that come from another place
    be forsaken?'—I'm on my way
    up to a wind-swept place
    of darkness, snow, and some lights, and further on
    a granite cave, icy water on its walls
    black flecked with white and pink, the good
    lair dark I dream to; start down fresh from.

from The Green Cape

*

—evergreens gravely
flourish below the fog
    —on the beach the gulls stand
    in disreputable looking groups
    and appear to be waiting
    stupidly for something

    but fly alone, intelligently

—where we were this morning
greens springing out
above other greens,
greens against greens
spear points, rays,
ribs, arcs of green

    (ocean makes a hush-hush
    hush   hush   sound
    with varying rumbles
    under it: the sound
    looms inland . . . .)

        *

—listen: in back of the rain forest
on a cold flat shining loop
of the river are some old logs
abandoned I suppose long ago
by a lumber company, and on the logs floating
near the bank, long grass was growing

        *

—at a rotting trunk we pause—I see
you noticing with well open
steady eyes what is to be seen:
in the one place alone
grow various mosses, three kinds of vine,
a mushroom, several smallish plants
with prettily cut leaves, and numerous
pine seedlings, inch high sprigs;
a flourishing of distinctions
in the same air, the same
half light

                    *

—yesterday (another yesterday), upcoast a few miles;
edge down a tall cliff to a sandy and stony isolated beach;

huge rocks, black in the offshore glitter, form islets, close
      set;
holes like doorways or gates eaten through them to
      sea-light;

sea lions loafing out there at water's edge, seafowl gray-
      white on crests;
the place is not of the land (which is shut off from it by
      the cliff);

the sea is shut away from it by the great rocks standing
      offshore;
the place is unfrequented by people; a violent cold wind
      is blowing:

      behind a black rock that rises
      straight up out of the beach

we encounter a collection
of huge stumps and logs,
each one weighing tons,
lodged everywhichway
(showing the strength
of the waves: how light-seeming
the logs would have spun
and tumbled in end over end)
their bark taken off cleanly
by storm, glare, wave-blow
they have acquired a sheen
of curious fineness—transmuted,
a silvery white, they
are phenomena of light,
LIGHT (that were never
formed to be in the light
living under moist bark
on a green slope somewhere)
now in their casual magnitude
and stillness they seem of the gods,
seem like the white bulls of a god
driven into this place between cliffs
and sea, and possessing it
now in the repose of their might

Desert

This bad country in the late afternoon wears us down,
The rocks with their dead purples,
The scabby cactuses, trees with tiny oily leaves

And thorns so big they're visible from the road,
Shrubs that look made out of old wire. Finally it all says:
That hard life of yours couldn't live out here, the bad country

Would free you of it; then the spirit, turning
Ruthless as it was in the days of the anchorites,
Could have a respite and stand empty on some hillside.

One Morning

The white
Of her flowers against the white sunlit wall
Is excellent indeed to contemplate

And
Similarly
Her silence

Inside
The prosy silence
Of the house.

Balances

How strong the young tree is, and heavy
    for standing so easily, and
    so readily shaking and bending
    in the light air

The small limb I saw at, drops and swings
    behind me unexpectedly and claws
    a rip in my shirt in passing ponderous and
    quick as a bear

As It Happens

It was in early middle age
That I saw for the first time
The legendary event—
Fresh water entering salt;
A creek came out from under
Darkness of pines and firs
Then down a stony beach
Pouring still crystalline
Among brown sand and stones
To the silent shock of entry
In a fogged, booming ocean,
Grays, grays and muffled whites,
Vague parallels hurrying in,
Creek shooting under, straight in.

Various Presences

Coming back to the house through the dark
I see a flashlight come on
at the dark window of Tim's room—
as I enter he trains it on me
and greets me.

He has climbed out of his bed
to look at some tomato worms again
which he put in a can today with fresh tomato leaves
fragrant with the scent
of tomatoes themselves—
he explains: he could hear the worms
chewing the leaves in the dark,
he imitates the sound for me,
a slight sucking sound.

The broad scars or scabs
on tomatoes are made, I suppose,
by these worms. We sit a moment
watching them in the flashlight beam.

Big fellows, a clear, light green,
built high and rectangular
like boxcars, and with a thorn
like a rose thorn set in their hind ends;
on their flanks are stripes,
diagonal, crooked, black, with white edging;
between each stripe is an imitation eye—
we look at it, it looks back at us,
a clear black pupil
rimmed with a delicate white tissue

that makes the eye appear to glisten
with moisture. The expression, we decide,
is that level, considering regard
you meet in the eye of a toad
or a lizard.

The Dragon of Things

1.
Silver Creek isn't silver
but dark, for the water flows, clear and shallow,
on a bed of black lava,

that flowed in its time,
thick and slow, over a sandstone bed that in its time
was slowly drifting sand.

Firs, cedars, and maples
shadow the thin soil that formed in time
upon the lava

—shadow Silver Creek
(among the shadows the streaks and blobs of light
are silver indeed) . . . .

2.
Where the lava flow stopped
the stream wore a gorge in the sandstone in time,
over the gorge hangs

the lava lip or ledge
from which the little stream drops free to its pool
among the rocks:

3.
Water entering air
is elementary, something important but not interesting
except as belonging

back among elementary things
and here having come forward, separated out
at the heart of the scene,

a violent exception
that sustains itself, making the uproar of the time that is
at the heart of the scene,

a "local dragon" sustaining
its presence in quiet start, loud close, and varying descent
all taking place at once,

hung timeless in time,
medium of the timeless—time taking its course,
gathering speed

in effortless accelerations
the dragon (tail gripping the ledge) arched out in the
    hissing pour,
scales streaming in heavy gouts,

U shaped, pulling apart
in threads, spatterings, whitening all over as at top speed
it enters the uproar

where, inside the bouncing spray,
among overlapping explosions and thudding sounds, the
    head
moves quietly from side to side,

at his distance. The dragon
in the falls is a kind of summary, and like the rainbow
in the spray it is vivid

161

with an intrinsic distantness. . . .
Beware the Dragon, I tell myself, as we are entering
the outskirts of the mist and din.

4.
On the spray-slick rocks,
we watch the thing once more. How slowly it bends
at the top, then parts

as it leaves the basalt shelf
into heavy strands that speed up promptly and start to
    tear apart
losing shape as they push harder

into the air, falling faster and faster
and in your last glimpse dropping like lightning,
    headlong,
disintegrating into the roar.

Fast as it happens, you can watch it
all the way down; you feel yourself involuntarily jerking
    back
at the last moment,

when the water goes on to smash itself
among rocks invisible but for a dark place now here, now
    there,
that suggest the snout swaying—

vivid with your attentive presence
at the danger, the near-far roaring of the dragon (or say
    heavy
machinery) back in the nature of things. . . .

Late February

The man down the creek owns a fruit tree
on which the white blossoms have just appeared
directly on the bare, red wood; how
they shine against the tree shadows
behind them—unaware that they are classic
Chinese plum blossoms . . . their owner
is idle, white haired, and in manner
unlike the people in the plum blossom
poems: he nods to me with a look that says
he knows something about what I think
(which is not the fact), when in the evening
he saunters past with his basset hound.

Memorial Bronze

I.
Strong cold gusts rake the ridge;
I drive into the east light;
The roadside wild oats shake,
Glisten delicately
—Silver for a girl's wrist.
But here sea haze to right,
Mountain chasm to left,
Against their small clearness.

II.
Miles, and nobody, then
Two helicopter crews,
Machines idling nearby,
And this whole back country
Seems theirs—they criss-cross it
As they please, their faces
Interested, easily
Looking out over it.

III.
More miles, and I wonder
Am I lost? A deer stands
Quietly in the road,
A flowering up, it seems,
Of the dust of the road
At just this moment,
And the road itself wild.
The deer walks off, down the slope.

IV.
Down steep, tight curves, jolting.
A strange rattle starts up
In the steering column.
Mudholes from the oozings
Of roadside springs. And there,
The shine of the river
Winding in the open
Valley. And no one down there.

V.
Much of that day is gone,
Half careless as I was
Of it—since it was mine,
I chose that, rather than
Become cautious with it;
So, much of it's well gone—
Into my bones, maybe;
Certainly out of reach.

VI.
Sycamores and alders,
Grass turning a bright brown;
In the vertical light
The loud water ablaze,
Skimmed by green-backed swallows—
Hawk, black in the distance,
Calling down at it all—

Now from these I recall
　　How in the unknown

River with nothing
Promised came the jolt
And quiver of the
First trout (thereafter
How readable were
The pools and riffles!)—
How then I kept on
Fishing past lunch time
Knowing the fatigue
This would mean; then ate
Somewhat hurriedly
At last with my boots
On a log to dry—
How I went downstream
Barefoot, astonished
By the pain! each small
Rock made its own pain—
How slowly that pain
Drove back the idea
Of a pleasant walk
Barefoot to that pool
Downstream; how I caught
Two fine trout while each
Move I made meant pain;
How the log had spurs
On it, like pinpoints,
Entering my bare feet
When I came back; how
In midafternoon,
Tired, I took my last
Good trout, at a bend
In dark blue shadow,
Under a rock ledge;

How then I rested
In some tall grasses,
How they hissed loudly
With the gusty wind
While I on the ground
Lay in still air; how
I thought of sleep, slept;
And woke in changed light,
Glare and shadow strange
On the water—late
Afternoon now! How
Fishing back upstream,
Seeing the water
From the other way—
Alien—chilled me;
How in my fatigue
I went by riffles
I'd have fished before;
How in that estranged
New-shining water
I caught two more trout,
And leaving them cleaned
On a streamside rock,
Turning back found one
Moved—then saw the snake
That moved it, his jaw-
joints unfastened, whole
Head of fish inside
His mouth, his own head
Startlingly deformed,
Eyes looking close-set
Now that the small head
Had been stretched so wide:

How, motionless, he
Watched me, knowing well
That I might kill him,
How his eyes asked, "Well,
Will you?" and waited;
How, as I held still,
He moved, ever so
Slightly, stealthily,
Looking right at me,
Which made me ashamed
For him—that he should
So deceive himself,
Pretend I was gone
While he saw me there;
How I went upstream
And from weariness
Lost three lures in quick
Succession, thinking:
I'm skin-tight, aching
With this day, bone-cracked
By it, like my friend
The snake with my trout
All but disabled
By the good fortune.
—Time to crawl home, then,
And sleep it off. How
A big, bushy tailed
Ruddy coyote paused
On a stony spur
And watched me a moment
As I drove toward him
On the road out; how,
Truth to say, the sight

On my return, of wife
And sons distressed me,
—I distressed myself
Among them, come back down
As I was, unfit
For human converse,
Drunk with the dry, bright
Liquor of the day.

from The Heat Lightning

I.   First twenty-four hours

7:00 P.M.
On the side to the west, with the light
of the low sun striking squarely
on the flat of the leaves,
the old cottonwood sparkles like a pond.

12:00 midnight
(There is nothing here, says the midnight,
but the lineaments of the real, resort
and support of every implication.)

2:00 P.M.
Surrounded by the hot fields the Russian Olives
make a brightness, growing along the draw—
the gray-green boughs are as clumps of frost
to the heart's desire that sees itself entering
that foliage from the heat and the light
as deer step into a grove and break up in shadows.

II.   Tree Meditation

In this country, of the few
native trees the commonest
is the cottonwood. Settlers
planted it for windbreaks, for
shade; it grows in giant rows
on irrigation ditches,
and stands over the houses
shading them in the summer
all day; it grows in the draws
and in great dark glittering
groves on the North and South Platte.

It takes the classic tree shape—
a round symmetrical crown,
a trunk short and straight and thick;
up close, you see that the leaves
grow in loose swinging bunches
out on the periphery—
the interior is gaunt
and the few major branches
form powerful, still arches
that contrast with the quick leaves
throwing off sharp bits of light.

Considered thus, the whole thing
suggests perception combined
with imperviousness. But
I turn to one specimen:
viewed up close its old trunk
with its deep rough crevices
and hard ridges covered with

sharp protuberances is
a badlands: there's nothing here
to penetrate to, it says;
impassive, unmoving, dead.

Whereas the leaves, with their fine
patterns and movements that take
the eye are transitory
and expendable—thousands
of them in agitation
all over, to the one trunk
almost featureless and like
nothing that's alive, whereby
the tree lives—holds out and lasts,
standing over the big ditch
steady and astir also.

The brown water runs past it
in the summer; in late fall,
the ditch dry and the weather
dry, the leaves turn a brilliant
clear yellow—it is startling,
the rough shining globe against
the clear sky. The leaves fall then
in the ditch and are still bright
and new-looking when the snow
covers them, below the wood
that stands patient in the air.

The tree has had its full growth
for some thirty years at least,
bears its multitudes of seeds
regularly—small white dots

in cotton that expands vaguely
and goes aloft on breezes,
looking supremely idle,
to drift up against fence posts
and weeds and along the sides
of farm buildings and upon
the crops, irrelevantly.

The tree having grown from one
white dot, you know that of course
on the microscopic scale
in the seed's interior
it worked as distinctively
as it does here, fully grown—
below those microscopic
particulars, well below
the molecular, there lay
at last vagueness, though; vagueness
is ultimate. Thence it came,

thither doubtless it will go;
but here it stands out clearly
against a sky, it traffics
with the world intricately
and persistently, fastened
by many ways into things;
moving to the world's movements
its cotton drifting thickly
through the air on certain days
in midsummer is a sight
ordinary and solemn.

I spend half an afternoon
underneath this glistener:

in a light breeze the leaves make
a fine pattering sound, like
gravel sliding down a slope;
if the breeze strengthens, the sound
becomes a voluminous
general hissing; stronger still,
and the hissing becomes a
roar of massive excitement—
as if a cyclone had struck.

All of these sounds are the sounds
of her present, passing, while
her trunk and limbs, hard things, dream
permanently, beneath sound
the dream of the air and rock
and water, things around in
inorganic splendor.—Now
from the leaves I can tell how
at its quietest the air moves
in eddies, isolated
short currents, streams with dead spots . . .

I single out one leaf: it
begins to tremble, then wags
violently. The breezes
start, quit, and start up again
all afternoon. The musings
of the tree, on one calm day.
Now agitation up high;
below, not a leaf moves. Now
a breeze pours through the whole tree
and it rattles—the polished
leaves clash stiffly together.

Is all this movement purely
decorative. Is a leaf
normally agitated,
or still; or is this movement
needful to the tree's workings.
Are the movements troubles. Or
merely the life of the tree—
neither necessary nor
irrelevant; its queenly
life—not indifferent;
its impartial experience. . . .

Three times I had the same dream
about this tree, in boyhood.
But I must explain—the trunk
for all its harshness, its lack
of fine structure, mere rocky
crevices and ridges, still
was vulnerable, of course—
a fungus got into it
near the point where the branches
arch up—the bark turned spongy
and brown, a depression formed.

The affliction seemed to me
dangerous; I was distressed.
A fluid like clean water
seeped from the place. Yesterday
when I examined the trunk
I saw clearly, down one side,
the stain left by the fluid;
though the spongy depression

had largely healed some time since,
in one spot I found some wet
soft bark; it smelt like moist earth.

That is the site of the dream.
I approach and a cavern
slopes upward into the huge
interior of the tree.
At the threshold I look up
and see on the crest in light
(a regular, clear numbus),
a great deer standing quietly;
in the cave's natural dark
the deer's wholly visible.
It looks at me; its eye shines.

I have no inclination
to approach any closer;
according to the dream's plan
I've had a look at my life,
which is all I was to do—
that was the feeling at first;
then the sense of the dream changed—
the deer was merely life
itself being presented
in repose for a moment
so that I could look at it.

So the tree stirs readily
in my mind—stirred yesterday
when I saw some of its kind
being felled a mile westward,

the great sections of the trunks
and limbs like fallen big game
in Africa—great females
slain and strewn about. But what
is this but an incident—
I drove past the summer day
they fell in a solid world.

Underneath the tree, grasses—
blue-stem, wild rye. A kind of
sharp-edged grass bends evenly,
as if combed, over the bank
of the ditch, trailing its tips
in the brown water. Woodbine,
planted by a bird-dropping,
doubtless, grows here—it would come
from an old vine in the yard,
set out by some grandparent.
It is flourishing in here.

A pretty place. The milkweed
is blooming—clusters of dull
or dead pink flowers, spikey
petals set on a flesh-like
protuberance, a hole
opening in the center
shaped like a five-pointed star;
the sweet odor's attracting
not only bees but ants—large
black ants with legs that raise them
high off the ground. On the road,

close, cars pass. In the grass lie
small branches shed by the tree;

the bark on some has loosened
and come off with the passage
of the seasons, and the wood
is bleached out. A few of these
look like antlers. As I turn
to examine one of them
a funeral procession
passes—black Cadillacs, then
a long line of every-day cars.

They bear the dead and mourning
to the new cemetery
put in just beyond this farm—
the mourners preoccupied
matter-of-factly. I feel
like waving to them, but check
the impulse. The tree stands on
this thirty foot strip of ground
between the road and the field;
beyond now, is not only
the graveyard but new houses.

So the traffic is heavy
on a road which in my youth
was silent, usually—
three or four cars going by
during a morning, perhaps.
Coming across on this ground
from the road, through the blue-stem,
to see the wild geraniums,
I came close to cutting my foot
on a beer bottle fragment.

Still it is a pleasant place.
I notice along the base
of the great trunk a blackened
area—from an old weed fire,
I suppose. There is a weed
whose name I don't know—dark green,
tall, it too is blooming now—
greenish-white little flowers
in closely set clusters like
clover-blossoms.—Sacred ground,
as our life is not; and ground

inevitably profaned;
maybe inexhaustible,
too, in its way.—Yesterday,
cutting into a seed pod,
prodding it with the knife point,
hunting for the small white seeds,
trying to find some pattern,
I saw this small white spider
emerge from the packed cotton
and, while I watched, go racing
away across the table.

III.   Elegy: The Old Man

Edging between the truck
and the wall I work back
to the far end, past the concrete,
onto the original dirt—
triangles of broken glass
shine among the old straw;
I make out a hame-ring,
yellowed and fly specked; a mended
strap, cracked and with salt
from dried sweat still on it; high
on the wall, hung there
perhaps by my brother, to be visible
and out of the way,
an old 'silver'
harness buckle, a heart shape
set in the center, catching
the half light where it bulges—
a bit of the bold old
finery of a set of harness.

I take it down. The heart is starred
with corrosion, dented on one side—
the whole buckle's bent awry,
across the concave underside
a spider has stretched a web:
in the quiet I can hear
the strain and give of the fabric
as I poke at it . . . nothing
underneath but a trace of fine
reddish dirt. I blow it out.

Regarding in the half-light
the heart's convexity, I consider
(in the heart's half-light)
taking the piece home with me. . . .

The buckle and such scraps
are like the notions surviving
in the gaunt, brittle, half-dark
interior of an old man
and the barn an old man
lasting into this other world
maybe in a subdivision
in California: he has come out
to live with one of his children,
and runs the power mower
once a week. He actually
cuts the grass, the barn
really shelters a truck;

the old man finds himself
wearing a sportshirt,
the barn is carrying
in its inner flank a stack
of spare grease-gun cartridges.
The barn still holds the smell
of harness leather, and manure,
and feed and the like—faint,
dry, distant, the fragrance
persists like the manner
of an earlier day in the speech
of the imaginary old man.

My sons may never know
how satisfactory a place
a barn is to take a leak in,
and this is a barn, since you can still
do so in the brown half-light,
the comfortable seclusion
—as for the dead in here
I think of them long since busy
at burying their own, as I make my way
back out, towards the day-glare.

IV.   The Summer

The birds keep to their routines.
The big cottonwood glitters.
In the approaching heat
of the middle of the day
the elm makes little movements
like a dozing horse.

On a distant county road
the sun bangs for an instant
on a windshield, flashing
like a signal; no reply.

A butterfly,
yellow with black
ribbing and trim, works the air
in between the house and trees,
disappearing from time to time
around the corner of the house
or inside one of the trees,
reappearing abruptly.

I come out after breakfast
every day, and sit writing
in the morning shade. Clear hours.
Butterfly's in the foreground
frequently; tall dusty weeds
by the road; then house, tree, field,
in the middle distance; then
the vapory pale mountains.

If I look up from my page
the butterfly is often
the one moving thing in sight.
I watch him rise at the end
of a glide with a broken,
tottering movement, working
his way up to a high bough
then not alighting, but merely
poising in the air;
then he veers off briskly.
He's not after anything.
A kind of extract of this
place, having worked free, he stays;

his apparently hesitant
turning this way and that is
just delighted watchfulness.

Afternoons he spends mainly
resting. And nights
on a weed stem, I suppose,
stiffening with the night chill,
the stem knobby with dew when
the morning sun first strikes it.

from Between Matter and Principle (1963)

My Friend the Motorcyclist

Like you I have shunned unrest
by moving, drawn up into
my matter, engrained and tough,
to force a future: my past
was that matter; blank air drew
over the blank, fearless stuff.

If I drove deep into fear
of blankness, what indifferent
principle stopped me, beside
the quiet road? Dry and clear
in the wind, some chance weeds spent
their pitted and wrinkled seed.

To be dislodged in minute
hard scatterings alien
to my hot intents, I found
was the principle, and brute
the miscellaneous man
dwindling down the road to town.

One of the Mantises

"Homer, who was a poet of war, . . . knew it was the
shield of such happiness as is possible on earth."
                                    —Santayana

The trim three-cornered head,
the body brought to an elegance
of elongations, the spiked

and heavy forearm tipped with
a surgical hook for the distracted
or the inattentive—in sandalwood

and light green his parts are one
deadly sanctity, twig-like
among the overlapping leaves.

Outside the House, Under Moonlight

Surviving their own depths and bounds
The rooftops of the neighborhood
Seem to have suddenly drawn near—
Over the blanched and molten grounds
Where boulders and old peach trees stood
The shapes look papery. Up the air

The moon, clean cinder of a blast
Whose glare is neither day nor night,
Has entered, violent and still
Driving the substance from a past—
My carnal mind goes like a bright
Haze on chill surfaces. A chill

Sleep can acknowledge best the might
That set loose these dead essences
Of what by day came steadily on
Then hunched in evening's slackened light—
Sleep (till we enter, like old trees,
The fresh restrictedness of dawn).

A Cedar

Look at me here. I stand
And grow still more the same
On this low hill of sand,
Compacted with my name.

This is my agony.
And blizzards cannot break
These boughs I build to be,
In weathering, awake.

Far down the August light,
Clouds form and shift at ease;
They're not free either, yet
Edge me in distances.

Come closer—touch my bark,
Smoke-silver and so thin
Your nail can shred it; dark,
The heartwood's just within.

Now you've begun, go on.
I am. I cannot mean,
Mere growth. Have me cut down,
Caught in a motive, seen

In, say, a little chest,
Rip-sawed, cross-cut, and planed
For a small good, to last,
Stopped, in a living end,

Disclosed by changeless lines,
Lampglow on my deep red;
Have among your designs
My minor fragrance freed.

Prologue: Moments in a Glade

Abiding snake:
                        At thirty-four
By unset spirit driven here
I watch the season. Warily
My private senses start to alter,
Emerging at no sign from me
In the stone colors of my matter.

You that I met in a dim path,
Exact responder with a wrath
Wise in conditions, long secure,
Settled expertly for the kill
You keep a dull exterior
Over quick fiber holding still . . .

Rocking a little, in a coarse
Glitter beneath fine, vacant space,
The hillside scrub oak interlocked
Where year by year, and unattended,
And by abrasive forcings raked
Against itself, it had ascended.

And yet below me sixty feet
A well of air stood dark and sweet
Over clean boulders and a spring.
And I descended through a ripple
Of upper leaves, till noticing
That a rock pattern had grown supple,

And whirred, I quietly backed off.
I have considered you enough.
The rattle stopped; the rigid coil,

Rustling, began to flow; the head,
Still watching me, swayed down to crawl,
Tilting dead leaves on either side.

You in the adventitious there,
Passion, but passion making sure,
Attending singly what it chose
And so condemned to lie in wait
Stilled in variety—to doze
Or wake as seasons fluctuate,

Eyes open always, the warm prey
At best but happening your way.
And I too slowly found a stone
To break your spine; and I have known
That what I will have surely spoken
Abides thus—may be yet thus broken.

193

from The Sum (1958)

A Walk in the Void

I could not see the life I live.
Wheeling to catch it as it was,
I found myself the fugitive;
There were my footprints, in reverse.
I could not praise them, could not curse.
Bare of their principle and cause,

They lay caught fast within that realm
No inquiry can justify,
No good or evil overwhelm.
To enter was to be interred
Where the gross lip absorbs the word.
It was what dead men occupy.

Or so it seemed. And yet I live.
Living I left my tracings there.
Driven historian, I arrive
Here where I blindly went, and see.
Dark walker through dubiety!—
Resuming you I grow aware,

Which is my life. O formless ground
Of quick experience, but not
Experience itself, I found
That I had walked upon your void
Saved by the blindness I employed
Till I stood blinking in my thought.

The Baby Cockatrice

I'd read of the vast reptiles, maybe seen
Some musty drawings of them, years ago.
The rumor that such creatures have once been
Will make a child fear, idly, *They are, now*.

Preoccupied and happy, I had fished
Well through a June day on Commotion Creek
And had my limit; now the water rushed
In shadow, mostly. Almost at the lake

I climbed the bank, tired, quiet. There he was.
He happened; total; there. He barely lay
A finger long—bone mouth and ruff and claws,
The plated body, and, shock on shock, the eye.

And once I turned, all I had been stayed there
Whole in a gaze where no more could occur.

The Daimon's Advice

So you of the slow-changing room
That each day you had wakened in
To be your own, provisional,
Slyly-known fellow, tried the sill,
Slipped out, renounced what you had been,
To tamper with this sourceless calm.

How long ago? you ask. But time,
The even circling round a center,
Has nothing here to circle through.
Where movement's neither false nor true,
To turn is not to leave, or enter,
But to stand, tenser yet, the same.

No, you must practice unconcern.
It will not do to glare, and call
Thunder to break from lightning-crack
That the world, at once, come densely back—
You'll owe to some stray, prose detail
Your unremarkable return.

The Death of a Buffalo
(out of Parkman)

Heavily from the shadeless plain to the river
The bull slants down and bends his head to draw
Bright water in, that goes unbroken ever.
He pauses, water threading from his jaw,
Impenetrably as he is, and old.
And, while the harsh beard drips and shines, the shore,
Beyond, grows flashing grasses. Through the cold
Water he lifts a foreleg, as before,
Showing the naked spot the ball drives through.
A shiver. The coming hour, the windy grass
Under the suns beyond him, these he knew,
Knows and shall know. They make no shift to pass
   Through death. Death is the elsewhere, an unwit
   Of the great body down, this side of it.

Valediction
under a lamp

The hot inrush of sensation
bursting to appetite, at once
fills and empties expectation,
unstoppable; as, for one who hunts,
invisible animals running
ahead of him through dripping trees
immobilized in clear morning
draw him through more than he can seize.

But a chill, as from touch denied,
comes with the weakening of light
for the morning hunter when wide
evening empties from his sight
the flashes of shapes, the colors
extracted confused from the air
past the earth, as the light lowers
deepening and vanishing there.

But homeward, the lamp is candor,
is the clear condition that flows
bodiless, through every color;
on the mobile knower it throws
the changeless beam, so that to know
by its remote intensity
is to regard the knowing, slow-
gathering, of its own laws, free:

ice-crystals will form themselves so
in a December night, if the wind
ceases, there is clear cold, and no
animal, harsh as accident,

crashes the water out of thirst—
but the beast may come; and the calm,
the cold, those negatives, that nursed
the ice, wait upon what will come.

And for the knower fresh time comes.
Knowledge is a farewell; sated,
remote as centerwood, it numbs;
may gather, as tree-rings, weighted,
motionless under the vital sheath—
till it all leans, then drops, dumb,
through temporal tremblings beneath,
extinguished, in completed calm.

The Vanishing Act
(for T. G.)

After he concluded that
he did not wish to raise his
voice when he spoke of such mat-
ters as the collapse of the

Something Empire, or of things
the folk suffer from, he sim-
ply set in words such meanings
as were there, and then, when he

finished the final verse, van-
ished in the blank below it:
he'll reappear only on
the next page (not written yet).

Small Song

"Turn on the hose," I say.
I kneel down on my lawn
To watch the water play.

At the depression where
The tree is set, it fills,
Transvisible as the air,

To level, tentative,
Then, trembling, overbreaks.
Its boundaries always give

Where the clear instants slow.
I stand, walk toward my house.
Shade slips. Place is aflow.

"You Need a Change of Scene"

Sick of the slippery rot old oaks beget,
The spongy browns of a summer sunken, wet
Leafy destructions, all the heavy smell,
The heavy going of the trees to hell,
I thought of the desert—sand, merely, and air,
The white region of sun, brilliant, bare,
In all directions blank simplicity. . . .
Good lack I sought, have I come close? I see
The wiry greasewood; scrub; pale trees whose trunks
Choke off in mistletoe; the riddled chunks
Of cactus snapped, or, leaning, hovering rife
With angry dying trapped in angrier life—
But nearer, now, the sun burns sure and bare,
Sure because bare. Let his stare be my stare.